CASE STUDIES IN SPECIAL EDUCATION

CASE STUDIES IN SPECIAL EDUCATION

A Social Justice Perspective

Edited by

TERA TORRES, ED.D.

and

CATHERINE R. BARBER, PH.D.

CHARLES C THOMAS • PUBLISHER, LTD.
Springfield • Illinois • U.S.A.

Published and Distributed Throughout the World by

CHARLES C THOMAS • PUBLISHER, LTD.
2600 South First Street
Springfield, Illinois 62704

ISBN 978-0-398-09173-6 (paper)
ISBN 978-0-398-09174-3 (ebook)

With THOMAS BOOKS *careful attention is given to all details of manufacturing
and design. It is the Publisher's desire to present books that are satisfactory as to their
physical qualities and artistic possibilities and appropriate for their particular use.*
THOMAS BOOKS *will be true to those laws of quality that assure a good name
and good will.*

Printed in the United States of America
TO-C-1

Library of Congress Cataloging-in-Publication Data

Names: Torres, Tera., editor. | Barber, Catherine R., editor.
Title: Case studies in special education : a social justice perspective /
    edited by Tera Torres, Ed.D. and Catherine R. Barber, Ph.D.
Description: Springfield, Illinois : Charles C. Thomas, Publisher, LTD.,
    [2017] | Includes bibliographical references and index.
Identifiers: LCCN 2017014437 (print) | LCCN 2017023733 (ebook) | ISBN
    9780398091743 (ebook) | ISBN 9780398091736 (paper)
Subjects: LCSH: Special education--United States--Case studies. | Special
    education--Social aspects--United States. | Social justice.
Classification: LCC LC3981 (ebook) | LCC LC3981 .C39 2017 (print) |
    DDC 371.90973--dc23
LC record available at https://lccn.loc.gov/2017014437

Artwork on front cover courtesy of Mr. John Romero (2017)

CONTRIBUTORS

Catherine R. Barber, Ph.D., is a licensed clinical psychologist and an Associate Professor in the School of Education and Human Services at the University of St. Thomas in Houston, Texas.

Katie D. Decatur, M.Ed., is an educational diagnostician and an experienced instructional leader. She is currently working as a literacy specialist in Southeast Texas.

Brenda Iveth de la Garza, M.Ed., is an educational diagnostician and an evaluation and education specialist in special education at Region One Education Service Center in Edinburg, Texas. She is also a doctoral candidate at the University of Texas Rio Grande Valley's program in Curriculum and Instruction with Bilingual Education Specialization.

Amy Ten Napel, M.A., is a specialist in school psychology with over 20 years of experience in the field of education. She is currently an education consultant providing professional development, consulting, and evaluation services through Total Special Education Solutions, LLC.

Kanisha Porter, Ph.D., is an Assistant Professor in the School of Education and Human Services at the University of St. Thomas. She works as an educational diagnostician in K-12 schools with research interests in decreasing special education identification.

Jannette Reyes, Ed.D., has worked in the field of special education since 1991. She has been providing professional development in the areas of Multicultural Education/Equity Literacy and Response to Intervention since 2003.

Helen S. Shaw, B.A., is currently completing a Master of Education in Teaching English to Speakers of Other Languages and a Master of Liberal Arts in International Studies at the University of St. Thomas. She has taught English in several countries and currently works at the University of St. Thomas as an academic advisor.

Corrie Staniszewski, M.A., is a speech and language pathologist. She worked in public schools for four years before transitioning to pediatric home health, where she currently practices.

Tera Torres, Ed.D., is an Assistant Professor at the University of St. Thomas and a certified educational diagnostician. She has been a special educator for over 15 years and has worked in both the private and public school systems.

Nicole McZeal Walters, Ed.D., is the Associate Dean of Graduate Programs and Assistant Professor of Educational Leadership at the University of St. Thomas. Her research agenda includes developing leaders to embrace culturally relevant leadership within P-20 education as it relates to equity and accountability, special and minority populations, and teacher training and development.

Griselda Landeros Wells, Ph.D., is a life-long educator of special needs children. She first started working in the field as a special education teacher and later as an Educational Diagnostician and a Licensed Specialist in School Psychology. She currently works as a Special Education Director.

ACKNOWLEDGMENTS

To the hills upon which I have died a slow and painful death (and you likely do not even know who you are): This is my offering to you. May you continue to resonate within my soul as a powerful force to be reckoned with so that I may be an agent of change rather than a part of the machine.

To my family: Why God gave you to me will always be a mystery. Despite all of the mistakes I have made in my life, God continues to love me enough to give you to me. Know that I love you to the ends of the earth. Andres, Hops, Jack, Cruz, Max, and Sam: We are Torres.

To my mother: I have no words. Love is not enough. Gratitude is not enough. You are a support system I need more than I will admit and I love you more than you will ever, ever know.

And to my co-editor and the authors included in this book: Thank you for doing this with me. Thank you for loving me and the kids included in the chapters enough to stand tall and speak up. We did it.

T. T.

To the three people who have taught me the most: Michael, Cecilia, and Fiona. You bring infinite joy and laughter to my life, and I love you beyond words.

To my first teachers—my parents, sisters, and brother—whose love, support, and friendship have given me the confidence to ask questions and challenge the status quo.

And to the wonderful teachers I have known who remind me what education *should* be: Ann, Kathy, Beverly, Sally, Elizabeth, Mandy, Katherine, Denise, Annie, Ely, and many more. Your work is a gift for which I am truly grateful.

C. R. B.

CONTENTS

TABLES AND FIGURES

CASE STUDIES IN SPECIAL EDUCATION

INTRODUCTION

Tera Torres, Katie Decatur, Corrie Staniszewski,
and Catherine R. Barber

From the early formation of the United States of America, children and adults with physical or mental impairments were considered to be of no benefit to society. In fact, these members of society were often barred from public places in general. A comprehensive historical review of the treatment of individuals with disabilities from the early 1600s to present (Neuhaus, Smith, & Burgdorf, 2014) indicated that there were residences set in place for those who were considered unable to contribute to the progression of society. Because there was no value placed on the lives of those living within these shelters, minimal effort was given to maintaining them. Abuse and neglect were common. Those with mental or physical impairments were afforded no civil rights and were often blamed for societal maladies such as poverty and crime.

Given this opinion of people with disabilities, it comes as no surprise that children with any type of disability were not included in the public education system. It was widely thought that physical or mental impairments would prevent a child from participating in any type of structured education. The public wanted to use as few resources as possible in caring for these devalued members of society. In the 1800s, this slowly started to change with a focus on the creation of at least some institutions for education of those with sensory disorders such as blindness or deafness. However, despite this sluggish movement forward, most children with disabilities still remained at home or in an institution, with only a small percentage of those children being educated privately if their parents had the means. However, by the mid-1900s, society was becoming more educated about physical and mental impairments, and social reform was taking place across the country.

Neuhaus and colleagues (2014) noted that as society changed its way of thinking, it worked to apply this change in a variety of ways to ensure fair treatment of individuals with disabilities, including within the educational realm.

One of the most important changes in the treatment of children with disabilities occurred when they were given the right to be educated by the public school system. Although states were initially encouraged to provide educational programs to children with disabilities through the passage of the Education of the Handicapped Act of 1970 (EHA; P.L. 91-230), this legislation was vague, and the interpretation of the law was left to the states (Martin, Martin, & Terman, 1996). However, current laws have specified that public education has the responsibility of ensuring equal opportunity within schools; that is, each child has the right to a free appropriate public education (FAPE) within the walls of any public school in America, and even access to some services provided at no cost if the child is participating in a private educational system. Yet the pursuit of equal opportunity for education regardless of ability is challenging, considering the wide range of mental and physical abilities that exist among children. The educational system needs to be able to accommodate a variety of individuals with a variety of needs, so special education continues to require refinement even today.

REVIEW OF EDUCATIONAL LEGISLATION

To grasp progression of the educational system and its current status, a review of relevant educational legislation is essential. The first major legislation aimed at improving success of students across the board was the Elementary and Secondary Education Act of 1965 (ESEA; P.L. 89-10), which emphasized that all students, regardless of socioeconomic status, should have equal opportunities and which began to set federal standards and accountability within public education. ESEA offered more equality with respect to educational opportunity for children who were economically disenfranchised and laid the framework for early special education laws. This Act marked the first time the federal government acknowledged an inequality in education. The Act was amended one year later and included two parts: (1) grant money was allocated to state education agencies for the creation of schools devoted to the education of children with special needs, and (2) Congress established the Bureau of Education of the Handicapped and the National Advisory Council for the benefit of students with disabilities. In 1968, this Act was amended again and established programs that supplemented the improvement of special education services.

As noted above, the federal government encouraged states to provide educational programs to children with disabilities through the passage of the Education of the Handicapped Act of 1970 (EHA); at this time, learning disabilities were established as a disability category. The Rehabilitation Act of 1973 (P.L. 93-112) is a critical piece of legislation because it addresses discrimination against people with disabilities. Specifically, this law includes Section 504, which is still used in public education today. Section 504 provides protection to all persons with disabilities; federal law defines a person with a disability as any person who "(i) [has] a physical or mental impairment that substantially limits one or more major life activities of such individual; (ii) [has] a record of such an impairment' or (iii) [is] regarded as having such an impairment. . ." (Americans with Disabilities Act of 1990, 42 U.S.C. § 12102).

In 1975, the Education for All Handicapped Children Act (P.L. 94-142) was passed. For the first time, reform for the education of children with disabilities was spelled out and required by law, a law that would guarantee that every child with special needs would have access to educational opportunity. The Education for All Handicapped Children Act of 1975 outlines the four main purposes of the law as follows:

1. to assure that all children with disabilities have available to them . . . a free appropriate public education which emphasizes special education and related services designed to meet their unique needs
2. to assure that the rights of children with disabilities and their parents . . . are protected
3. to assist States and localities to provide for the education of all children with disabilities
4. to assess and assure the effectiveness of efforts to educate all children with disabilities.
(EAHCA, 1975, Section 3a)

The Education for All Handicapped Children Act is a pivotal piece of legislation for special education. This legislation specified the need for a free appropriate public education (FAPE) for all children and protected the rights of children with disabilities and their parents. This act was also designed to assess the effectiveness of special education programs and offered federal financial assistance to all state and local education agencies for the education of children with disabilities. This law mandated Individualized Education Programs (IEPs) and Least Restrictive Environment (LRE) and ensured due process rights. In addition, efforts were made to improve the process for identifying and evaluating children with disabilities.

Before the passage of this act, many children with disabilities had zero access to any educational system, and the ones who did had limited, unregulated access that mostly focused on providing accommodations to children with disabilities rather than properly evaluating them and educating them according to their potential (U.S. Department of Education, 2010). While the Education for All Handicapped Children Act of 1975 specifically addressed the needs of children with disabilities, the 1983 amendment to the EHA (P.L. 98-199) gave additional weight to special education by adding incentives for preschool programs, early intervention programs, and transition services for children with special needs. In addition, the Office of Special Education replaced the Bureau of Education for the Handicapped. The 1986 amendment (P.L. 99-457) lowered the age of eligibility for special education services from age five, as specified by P.L. 94-142, to age three. These amendments also established the Handicapped Infants and Toddlers program, which directed early intervention programs for children from birth to age three. Under this program, the families of infants and toddlers with special needs could also receive assistance.

In 1990, the Education of the Handicapped Act amendments renamed the law the Individuals with Disabilities Education Act (IDEA; P.L. 101-476). Special programs for transition and for children with serious emotional disturbances were created, along with research programs for attention deficit disorder. IDEA 1990 also added autism and traumatic brain injury to the list of categories of children and youth eligible for special education and related services. The Handicapped Infants and Toddlers program was renamed the Early Intervention Program for Infants and Toddlers with disabilities.

The 1997 reauthorization of IDEA (P.L. 105-17) made some critical changes to the original Education of all Handicapped Children Act of 1975. The reauthorization required, among other things, a more specific and more descriptive Individualized Education Program (IEP) that would guide instruction. It also mandated that all children participate in statewide testing programs and increased the need for mainstreaming of children with disabilities.

In the early twenty-first century, two major pieces of education legislation were authorized; these would come to shape the current state of general and special education in the United States more than any previous legislation. First, the earlier Elementary and Secondary Education Act of 1965 was reformed into the No Child Left Behind Act in 2001. Second, the Individuals with Disabilities Education Act was reformed into the Individuals with Disabilities Education Improvement Act of 2004.

The No Child Left Behind Act of 2001 (NCLB; P.L. 107-110), a reauthorization of the ESEA, was passed by Congress in 2001 and signed into law in 2002. The law was originally created in an effort to make the United States more academically competitive at the international level. This involved increased regulation by the federal government to ensure that all students were achieving success, especially those who have traditionally struggled, such as children speaking English as their second language, children coming from lower socioeconomic settings, students from racial or ethnic minority groups, and children participating in special education. Over the course of time, this measure, which was widely supported by Congress across party lines, has become more controversial. The main focus of the law has been on standardized testing and adequate yearly progress, both of which are influenced by state-level interpretation.

There have been definite benefits as a result of this law. First, it recognized the subgroups that were having the most difficulty succeeding. Then it came up with solutions to try to increase academic success within those groups. This placed more emphasis on the monitoring of progress within these populations, most notably special education. The effects of NCLB have reached educators across the U.S., who, while feeling that NCLB was extremely hard if not impossible to implement, have also admitted that it makes it harder to "sweep kids under the rug" (Hussey, 2008, p. CT7). According to Hussey (2008), some schools have had to pay out of pocket to try to improve standards when unable to make adequate yearly progress, and this has motivated them to make changes. Yet despite this success, many educators still feel that overall, NCLB has been more harmful than helpful due an unrealistic expectation of achievement and the extreme focus on standardized testing that is used to measure that achievement (Hussey, 2008). Schools are held accountable for student success and are subsequently fined and potentially denied future funding if students are not successful, which NCLB defines as being proficient in reading and math. The impact on schools is profound, leading to school closures, budget cuts, and denial of funds for schools across the nation.

The other major piece of educational legislation, the Individuals with Disabilities Education Improvement Act (IDEIA) of 2004 (P.L. 108-446), stayed true to its original intent to provide FAPE for students with disabilities. The major changes addressed were summarized by Apling and Jones (2005) in their report for Congress:

- An extensive definition of highly qualified teachers
- Provisions for reduction of paperwork
- Extensive provisions ensuring special education for homeless and highly mobile populations
- Increased funds and requirements for statewide activities
- Authorization for states to use IDEA funds to establish and maintain "risk pools" for schools that provide high cost IDEA services
- Modifications to requirements for parents who opt to place their children in private schools
- Revised state performance goals and requirements for children's participation in state assessments with the goal of aligning these requirements with the ESEA of 1965
- Authority for increases in IDEA funds to off-set expenditures related to special education
- Authority to use IDEA funds for early intervening services
- Changes to procedural safeguards
- Major changes in compliance monitoring to focus on student performance
- Authority to extend Part C services for infants and toddlers beyond the age of 2. (p. 2)

In addition, new language in IDEIA acknowledged the challenges for students with English as a second language as those challenges relate to referrals, evaluations, and identification of such students with disabilities. Sections were added to recognize that students from racial and ethnic minority groups (whom we will hereafter refer to as "students of color," in keeping with *The American Heritage Guide to Contemporary Usage and Style*, 2015) are over identified, particularly in the eligibility categories of mental retardation and emotional disturbance. IDEIA requires that transition planning be incorporated for all students with disabilities to facilitate greater success with postsecondary goals and outcomes for such students. Also mandated is the notion that all students will participate in state assessment measures, and those measures are to be modified or accommodated and may include alternate assessments for students in special education. Parents are given the power to request initial evaluations for special education, and the timeline for obtaining informed consent is specified. In addition, consent for services must be obtained from the parent once the evaluation is completed prior to any services being provided. Furthermore, IDEIA now includes and provides for children in private schools who have been placed there voluntarily by their parents.

One of the biggest changes accompanying this reauthorization was the allowance for other measures of identifying learning disabilities. The discrepancy model, which defined learning disabilities as a significant gap between intelligence (as measured by IQ) and achievement, was essentially tossed, with preference given to intervention methods (i.e., Response to Intervention). Although this allowance gives evaluators greater flexibility for establishing (or disconfirming) a diagnosis, it also leads to potential confusion about the appropriate means of evaluating learning disabilities and opens the door for highly inconsistent assessment methods.

In 2015, the No Child Left Behind Act was renamed Every Student Succeeds Act (P.L. 114-95). With this reauthorization, states were given the flexibility to manage their own accountability systems in schools without the requirement that every child be proficient in reading and math. States were also encouraged to get rid of unnecessary testing and may use whatever methods deemed appropriate by the state itself, including SAT and ACT testing instead of previously used state assessments. States now have the autonomy to choose their own curriculum instead of being required to use what was previously federally mandated. In addition, schools can no longer be evaluated using test scores exclusively, and struggling schools will receive more federal funding to assist with improving student outcomes. This reauthorization also endorsed Universal Design for Learning, which is an educational "framework for understanding how to create curricula that meets the needs of all learners from the start" (Center for Applied Special Technology, 2011, p. 4). Finally, it is now required that parents are involved in the development of state education plans (U.S. Department of Education, n.d.).

As this timeline indicates, special education law—and, therefore, special education practice—has undergone profound transformation over a relatively short time span (50 years). Students with disabilities are now more likely to receive a free and appropriate public education in the least restrictive environment possible, with funding to support this. However, as we will show in subsequent chapters, the ideals of the law have not always been manifested in effective practice.

THE VALUE OF STORIES IN UNDERSTANDING SPECIAL EDUCATION

To the ancient Egyptians, storytelling was more than simply a means of passing on information; it was meant to preserve a way of life. Scientists study hieroglyphics for hours trying to determine how these people lived, where they worked, and what they ate. While we can certainly assess how many caves have hieroglyphic writing inside and how many different symbols there are, this quantitative information has little, if any, meaning unless it is viewed through a more qualitative lens. This requires hearing people's stories and trying to understand the meaning and implications of these stories.

As educators, we have found student narratives to be a much needed but poorly understood dimension of scholarship. While we may indeed be providing better educations and more services for children with special needs overall than we provided in the formative years of our public education system, we could be providing much more learning to all children if we had some real sense of who the children are. This idea of coupling a child's own narrative with the experiences and context of the current system is the focus of this book.

According to Connelly and Clandinin (1990), "humans are storytelling organisms who, individually and socially, lead storied lives" (p. 2). *Narrative,* or the telling and studying of stories, has a place across disciplines, as narrative is a uniquely and universally human experience. Our own stories as educators, evaluators, and psychologists do not stand alone; in fact, they do not exist without the stories of the students with whom we work.

According to Ochs and Capps (1996), "narrative and self are inseparable" (p. 19). In this book, we try to focus on the experiences of students and use those stories to shape and define our own sense of knowing that we can share with readers. It was out of our frustrations with policies and procedures that this book was born, and, C. Wright Mills (as cited in Bullough and Pinnegar, 2001) reminds us, "personal troubles cannot be solved merely as troubles, but must be understood in terms of public issues . . . human meaning of public issues must be revealed by relating them to personal troubles and to the problems of individual life" (p. 14).

NARRATIVE INQUIRY AS A METHODOLOGICAL FRAMEWORK

Narrative inquiry is a qualitative research method that involves a focus on people's lived experiences through the examination of their stories (Clandinin, 2006). Pinnegar and Daynes (2007) describe the narrative inquiry process as requiring a turn or shift from a more objective, distanced, and quantitative research stance to a more experiential, participatory, and qualitative research stance. Clandinin and Connelly (2000) call it "people in relation studying people in relation" (p. 189).

In the field of special education, particularly research devoted to evaluation of disabilities and achievement, it can be tempting to become overly focused on numerical data obtained through standardized assessments. Similarly, there is a strong pull to assess, categorize, and label, under the assumption that this can be done reliably and accurately if only the rules are followed. Perhaps this is why educators are given only 13 special education eligibility categories from which to choose. Children whose profiles fit these categories receive services and those who do not fit do not receive services. Such views and practices reflect black-and-white thinking, yet reality is rarely black and white. Every child is unique, and a single set of numbers obtained during a restricted period of evaluation rarely tells the child's whole story. This is where narrative inquiry comes in: We have to search beyond the numbers to understand children's experiences so that we can better help them.

Although traditional, quantitative educational research has immense value in its ability to tell us about the typical or average student and for providing a snapshot of a classroom, school, district, or state in terms of measurable outcomes, such data are incomplete. Accountability should be about more than just numbers; it must include a look at students' lives—are they actually benefiting from special education services? What are the unintended consequences of placement decisions? How do educators feel about their own role in the process? As individual children's, families', and educators' stories are shared, the power of the particular emerges. Narratives tend to linger within one's memory, and the lasting impression of such narratives is the driving force of this book. To this end, contributing authors have identified stories that come from their direct experience with the children involved. Those children's stories have resonated with chapter authors as ones that must be told in an attempt to rectify the current ways we handle special education in our public school system. Giving voice to these stakeholders is the first step in achieving social justice in education.

SOCIAL JUSTICE IN EDUCATION

The roots of social justice advocacy and reform in education date back to the early twentieth century, but the movement became much more widespread during the 1950s–1970s with the rise of de-segregation efforts and the introduction of bilingual education and multicultural education (Williamson, Rhodes, & Dunson, 2007). The literature on social justice in education is incredibly diverse, with no universally agreed-upon definition of social justice (Hytten & Bettez, 2011). Nonetheless, many social justice conceptualizations focus on core themes that reflect basic ethical and moral principles (Pilsner, 2012), such as the equal dignity and rights of all people (including children); people's shared responsibility for the common good; parents' rights and responsibilities with regard to their children's education; and the value of integral, humane education (i.e., one that develops all aspects of a child in a manner that respects his or her dignity). Based on these and similar principles, social justice proponents in education have advocated for increasing awareness of and working to eliminate oppression within the educational system, providing equal access to a high-quality education, and promoting human dignity by respecting and valuing individual differences (Landreman & McDonald-Dennis, 2013). All of these themes are relevant to the issues in the United States special education system that we have identified in the current book.

To capture these themes in a single framework, we have adopted Gewirtz's (2006) theory of social justice, which takes a multidimensional approach. Gewirz (2006), drawing on the work of Young (1990), has suggested that social justice is composed of three constructs: distributive justice, which entails the rules by which goods and cultural and social resources are distributed among members of a society; recognitional justice, which entails the presence of respect, recognition, and non-domination within a society; and associational justice, which entails opportunities for democratic participation and gives a voice to the disadvantaged (pp. 74–75).

Gewirtz's (2006) multidimensional conceptualization of social justice is appropriate in understanding the failures of the special education system for two reasons. First, if we were to focus exclusively on distributive justice, or justice as fairness (e.g., Rawls, 2001), some might argue that the current special education system is socially just. For example, current special education policy (IDEIA, 2004) mandates a free appropriate public education for all students, regardless of ability. Furthermore, the law authorizes additional funds, resources, and supports for students with disabilities, with a preference for providing education in the least restrictive environment. These fundamental tenets of special education certainly seem to fulfill popular social justice principles that all people have equal access to basic liberties (in this case, education) and that any inequalities benefit those who are most disadvantaged (in this case, students with disabilities). However, this one-dimensional perspective on social justice focuses exclusively on *access* to education and the presence of additional funds and resources. It ignores deeper concerns about the actual quality and outcomes of special education, issues of over and under identification, the stigma and differential treatment experienced by students with disabilities, and the relative lack of power that families and students themselves have in the special education referral and placement process. In contrast, a multidimensional theory of social justice that incorporates respect, recognition, and increased participation in decision-making better captures our ideals for a socially just special education system.

Second, Gewirtz's concept of associational justice emphasizes the importance of giving *voice* to those who are disadvantaged and marginalized. The case study approach that we use in this book gives voice to those students, families, and educators who have been let down by the special education process. Associational justice in education involves bringing those voices to the forefront so that others will hear and respond to them. That being said, in a discussion of nonviolent approaches to social justice in education, Wang (2013) has rightly noted that "social justice education needs to be attentive to its own tendency toward polarizing sameness/difference, self/other into irreconcilable or distant opposites in the existing discourses, assumptions, and practices" (p. 489). In the current context, this means that our efforts to bring special education students and their families in from the margins must not in turn marginalize the educators who have assumed the awesome responsibility of serving these students.

The goal of this book is not to castigate teachers, school leaders, or policy makers. Rather, the goal is to shed light on the flaws and injustices of the status quo. Having identified these problems, we then offer solutions. We hope that our approach will appeal to the minds and hearts of readers so that they will become advocates for change.

AN OVERVIEW OF
CASE STUDIES IN SPECIAL EDUCATION

There are three sections included in this book, and each section has chapters that correlate to specific themes. Although the themes are not exhaustive, they are representative of the issues faced by children interacting with the special education system. Section one is devoted to issues surrounding identification of students with disabilities, specifically learning disabilities and emotional and behavioral disorders. Chapter 1 addresses the issue that local education agencies are responsible for establishing their own eligibility criteria for identifying students with learning disabilities. The case of "Charles" elucidates the inconsistencies in assessment and diagnosis that often occur. Chapter 2 is dedicated to understanding the struggle of the slow learner. The case of "Karla" illustrates what happens to a student who fails to meet diagnostic criteria as a student with a learning disability because her underachievement is not "unexpected." The case suggests that failure to provide services to slow learners will likely result in negative outcomes for these students as they enter society as adults. Chapter 3 presents the case of "DJ," a behaviorally challenged student with a record of substance possession, truancy, and disrespect, who was left to "wait to fail." Students like DJ often do not have any access to behavioral supports or interventions despite their behavioral challenges interfering with their educational performance.

Section two of this book addresses problems within the evaluation process that negatively influence diagnosis. In Chapter 4, the case of "Shavonne" illustrates the impact of socioeconomic factors that

negatively affect educational performance. Although federal regulations list sociological factors as grounds for ruling out a diagnosis, these
factors are often overlooked. Chapter 4 also raises the problems of disproportionate representation of students from low socioeconomic
backgrounds and students of color within the special education system.
Chapter 5 addresses the problematic evaluation process for bilingual
students. The case of "Sonia," a student who was determined to have
no clear language dominance between Spanish and English, highlights
how the evaluation process often fails bilingual students. Chapter 5
also identifies numerous risk factors English Language Learners (ELLs)
face and describes how an appropriate intervention plan geared for
ELL students can improve their educational outcomes.

Section three highlights significant concerns with service provision
within the special education realm. Chapters 6 and 7 present two different but complementary viewpoints on the issue of Individualized
Education Programs (IEPs), specially designed instruction, and the
mandate that special education must be aligned to the grade-level curriculum and standards. Chapter 6 explains how educators are implementing IEPs in an effort to provide individualized instruction for
students in special education. In a push for more success on high-stakes
tests from the special education population, IEP goals are aligned with
grade-level standards, and progress is acknowledged only when a student meets one of the measurable goals on his or her IEP. Two cases
illustrate the pitfalls in IEP development and implementation: "Jamie,"
a child with severe autism, and "Mikah," a child with a speech impairment and other health impairment. Chapter 7 describes appropriate,
specially designed instruction for students with disabilities. Unprepared
educators are unable to provide specially designed instruction when
professional development and resources are lacking. This chapter illustrates a three-step process of specially designed instruction as applied
to three cases: "Aaron," "Jackson," and "Cody."

ELLs, students of color, and students with low socioeconomic (SES)
backgrounds make up a significant portion of special education referrals. Although Response to Intervention (RTI) has been a positive step
for improving the accuracy of identification, RTI is not always implemented with fidelity and thoughtfulness. With a lack of clearly defined
intervention procedures, educators experience a heavy focus on forms
and meetings with little attention provided to improving classroom instruction. Chapter 8 presents the case of "Jeremy" to discuss how

schools can improve results within a multi-tiered system of support with effective leadership practices.

THE STORY BEGINS

This book presents the stories of the children on the receiving end of severely fractured laws and misguided educational practices. The stories are raw and real, but all identifying information has been removed or altered to maintain confidentiality and privacy. Some material is difficult to read and shocking to absorb, and as authors, sometimes the only consolation has been that each child has a voice and each child's story is written down here for someone to read. The potential for these stories to change the status quo is great, and change is critically needed, especially when it comes to making decisions about other people's children.

Although the stories presented in this book are the primary focus, we felt that it was not enough merely to raise questions and challenge the status quo. We must also offer solutions. Each chapter contains practical, shorter-term solutions for educators, school leaders, and policy makers. In addition, the Conclusion presents our longer-term, unified vision for a more effective, evidence-based, and socially just special education system—one that is worthy of our country's children.

Who is speaking up for those children? Is anyone else screaming besides the children—anyone who has a voice loud enough to be heard? Who has the power to make change? Who has enough knowledge about the realities of special education, not just the rumors, to make judgments? This is where we have entered the playing field—as researchers, writers, educators, and practitioners. It is here that we focus our story of discovery, questioning the policies and procedures that dictate the systems currently in place in our schools.

REFERENCES

Apling, R., & Jones, N. (2005). *Individuals with Disabilities Education Act (IDEA): Analysis of changes made by P.L. 108–446.* (Congressional Research Service Report for Congress, Order Code RL32716). Retrieved from http://research.policyarchive.org/198.pdf

Americans with Disabilities Act of 1990, 42 U.S.C. § 12102. (2017).

Bullough, R. V., & Pinnegar, S. (2001). Guidelines for quality autobiographical forms of self-study research. *Educational Researcher, 30*(3), 13–21.

Center for Applied Special Technology. (2011). *Universal design for learning guidelines version 2.0.* Wakefield, MA: Author. Retrieved from http://www.udlcenter.org/aboutudl/udlguidelines

Clandinin, D. J. (2006). Narrative inquiry: A methodology for studying lived experience. *Research Studies in Music Education, 27,* 44–54.

Clandinin, D. J., & Connelly, F. M. (2000). *Narrative inquiry: Experience and story in qualitative research.* San Francisco: Jossey-Bass.

Connelly, F. M., & Clandinin, D. J. (1990). Stories of experience and narrative inquiry. *Educational Researcher, 19*(5), 2–14.

Education for All Handicapped Children Act of 1975, Pub. L. No. 94–142, 89 Stat. 773 (1975).

Education of the Handicapped Act Amendments of 1983, Pub. L. No. 98–199, 97 Stat. 1357 (1983).

Education of the Handicapped Act Amendments of 1986, Pub. L. No. 99-457, 100 Stat. 1145 (1986).

Education of the Handicapped Act of 1970, Pub. L. No. 91–230, 84 Stat. 121 (1970).

Elementary and Secondary Education Act of 1965, Pub. L. No. 89–10, 79 Stat. 27 (1965).

Every Student Succeeds Act of 2015, Pub. L. No. 114–95. Retrieved from https://www.gpo.gov/fdsys/pkg/BILLS-114s1177enr/pdf/BILLS-114s1177enr.pdf

Gewirtz, S. (2006). Towards a contextualized analysis of social justice in education. *Educational Philosophy and Theory, 38*(1), 69-81.

Hussey, K. (2008, Oct. 10). More schools miss the mark, raising pressure. *New York Times,* CT7. Retrieved from http://www.nytimes.com/2008/10/12/nyregion/connecticut/12nochildct.html

Hytten, K., & Bettez, S. C. (2011). Understanding education for social justice. *Educational Foundations, 25,* 7-24.

IDEA Improvement Act of 1997, Pub. L. No. 105-17, 111 Stat. 37 (1997).

Individuals with Disabilities Education Act of 1990, Pub. L. No. 101-476, 104 Stat. 1103 (1990).

Individuals with Disabilities Education Improvement Act of 2004, Pub. L. No. 108-446, 118 Stat. 2647 (2004).

Landreman, L. M., & MacDonald-Dennis, C. (2013). The evolution of social justice education and facilitation. In L. M. Landreman (Ed.), *The art of effective facilitation* (pp. 3-22). Sterling, VA: Stylus.

Martin, E., Martin R., & Terman, D. (1996). The legislative and litigation history of special education. *The Future of Children, 6*(1), 25–39.

Neuhaus, R., Smith, C., & Burgdorf, M. (2014). Equality for people with disabilities, then and now. *GP Solo, 31*(6). Retrieved from http://www.americanbar.org/publications/gp_solo/2014/november_december/equality_people_disabilities_then_and_now.html

No Child Left Behind Act of 2001, Pub. L. No. 107-110, 115 Stat. 1425 (2001).

Ochs, E., & Capps, L. (1996). Narrating the self. *Annual Review of Anthropology, 25,* 19-43.

Pilsner, J. (2012, February 13). Catholic social principles for education. [Letter to Robert LeBlanc, Dean, School of Education]. University of St. Thomas, Houston, TX.

Pinnegar, S., & Daynes, G. (2007). Locating narrative inquiry historically: Thematics in the turn to narrative. In D. J. Clandinin (Ed.), *Handbook of narrative inquiry* (pp. 3–34). Thousand Oaks, CA: Sage.

Rawls, J. (2001). *Justice as fairness: A restatement.* Cambridge, MA: The Belknap Press of Harvard University Press.

Rehabilitation Act of 1973, Pub. L. No. 93–112, 87 Stat. 355 (1973).

The American heritage guide to contemporary usage and style. (2015). Boston: Houghton-Mifflin.

U.S. Department of Education. (n.d.). Every Student Succeeds Act (ESSA). Retrieved from https://www.ed.gov/essa?src=ft

Wang, H. (2013). A nonviolent approach to social justice education. *Educational Studies, 49*(6), 485-503.

Williamson, J. A., Rhodes, L., & Dunson, M. (2007). A selected history of social justice in education. *Review of Research in Education, 31*, 195–224.

Young, I. M. (1990). *Justice and the politics of difference.* Princeton, NJ: Princeton University Press.

Chapter 1

TO BE (LD) OR NOT TO BE (LD)?
THAT DEPENDS

TERA TORRES

I believe that if we continue trying to define learning disabilities by using ill-defined concepts, we will forever be frustrated, for it is an illusive concept. We are being bamboozled. It is as though someone stated a great hoax by inventing a term then tempting others to define it. And lo and behold, scores of task forces and others have taken the bait. (Lovitt, as cited in Algozzine & Ysseldyke, 1987, p. 317)

INTRODUCTION

Because so many students with learning disabilities are being mainstreamed into general education classrooms, there is a strong and immediate need to juxtapose the needs of these students with the expectation that they learn, and subsequently perform on state-mandated achievement tests, in environments where teachers are inexperienced and ill-equipped to teach students with learning disabilities. However, prior to educating teachers about best instructional methods for teaching students with learning disabilities, some sort of consensus must be established, at least among educators, about what a learning disability really is. To that end, current legislation leaves much of the eligibility determination to the local education agency (LEA) itself, which is proving to be a challenge unlike ones seen previously in the field. Unfortunately, allowing LEAs to determine their own eligibility criteria creates and encourages inconsistent services and supports that are ultimately detrimental to the educational experience of the student and problematic for schools trying to provide said programming.

BACKGROUND

Evolution of the Definition of Learning Disabilities

In the early part of the nineteenth century, children with special needs were usually not formally educated. As formal education expanded and the public demanded access to education for all persons, children with special needs began requiring some attention. The notion of learning disabilities can be traced as far back as the mid-1800s, when Franz Joseph Gall began to suggest the existence of a relationship between mental impairment and brain injury (Hallahan & Mercer, 2002). Many theorists, psychologists, and physicians have attempted to explain what are now called learning disabilities using a medical model, including Dr. Samuel Orton who is credited as being the key figure in the diagnosis and treatment of reading disabilities in the United States. Dr. Orton worked in a psychiatric hospital and noted that many of the students in his program who had average or above average cognitive capabilities were also identified as having academic problems (Hallahan & Mercer, 2002). Though John Hinshelwood reported decades earlier that his patients with word-blindness were intelligent as well, Orton had the added benefit of IQ assessments to support the notion of intelligence. Orton also rejected Hinshelwood's idea that reading difficulties were the result of poor brain development; rather, Orton reported, reading difficulties were a result of sides of the brain working in a mirror fashion (Hallahan & Mercer, 2002). More specifically, Orton noted, cerebral cortexes of the brain were mixed up in that these children reversed the letters /p/ and /q/ and /b/ and /d/. They also mixed words such as "was" and "saw" and appeared to read from right to left (Hallahan & Mercer, 2002).

Samuel Kirk was next to play a crucial role in the development of research in the field of learning disabilities. A graduate student in 1929, Kirk encountered a boy labeled "word-blind" while working at a research institute. After spending seven months teaching the boy to read, Kirk had remediated the boy's skills to a third-grade level (Hallahan & Mercer, 2002). This was life changing for Kirk, as he had never heard of the term "word-blind" and later went to work at a residential facility for children who were mentally retarded, where ground-breaking work in the field of learning disabilities was taking place. The residential facility was called Wayne County Training School, and Kirk encountered many children with what would now be coined learning disabilities. It was in this setting that one begins to see the separation of children with mental retardation from children with what were later called learning disabilities. In a book published in 1972, Kirk offers his assertion about the nature of learning disabilities:

> . . . it generally refers to the problems of children who, although normal in sensory, emotional, and intellectual abilities, exhibit disorders in spoken and written language, including disorders in perception, listening, thinking, talking, reading, writing, spelling, or arithmetic. (p. 68)

It was Barbara Bateman, a student of Kirk's, who combined the IQ–Achievement discrepancy model with Kirk's definition:

> . . . an educationally significant discrepancy between their estimated potential and actual level of performance related to basic disorders in the learning process, which may or may not be accompanied by demonstrable central nervous system dysfunction, and which are not secondary to generalized mental retardation, educational or cultural deprivation, severe emotional disturbance, or sensory loss. (Swanson, Graham, & Harris, 2005, p. 22)

From this definition, the concept of learning disabilities became interwoven with what is now known as the discrepancy model. It was during the early 1960s that the idea took hold that such a disability exists so as to limit or impair a child's inabilities that is not related to mental retardation. In 1967, the National Advisory Committee on Handicapped Children (NACHC) provided a definition of a specific learning disability (that was later included in Public Law 94–142 in 1975):

> . . . a disorder in one or more of the basic psychological processes involved in understanding or in using language, spoken or written, which may manifest itself in an imperfect ability to listen, think, speak, read, write, spell, or to do mathematical calculations. The term includes such conditions as perceptual handicaps, brain injury, minimal brain dysfunction, dyslexia, and developmental aphasia. The term does not include children who have learning problems which are primarily the result of visual, hearing, or motor handicaps, of mental

retardation, of emotional disturbance, or of environmental, cultural, or economic disadvantage. (National Joint Commission on Learning Disabilities, 1991, p. 1)

This definition was used throughout recent history, though much controversy has ensued due to such a sociologically exclusive, but medically all-inclusive, one-size-fits-all approach to identification. McCormick (1995) writes that "learning disability" is a generic description that replaced several different labels to describe students who "had difficulty in listening, mathematics, reading, speaking, spelling, thinking, or writing" (p. 10). She asserts that learning disabilities now encompass children who, prior to the early 1960s, were described as:

> . . . brain-injured, developmentally dyslexic, dysgraphic, neurologically disordered, neurologically impaired, perceptually handicapped, psychoneurologically disabled, congenitally word-blind, childhood aphasics, cerebral dysfunctions, chronic brain dysfunctions, Strauss-syndrome, strephosymbolia. (McCormick, 1995, p.11)

As part of the Education of the Handicapped Act of 1970 (Public Law 91-230, Part G), Congress recognized learning disabilities as a formal disability category eligible for financial assistance, and money was allocated to the United States Office of Education (USOE) to provide for grants that support teacher education, research, and model service delivery systems with respect to learning disabilities (Bradley, Johnson, Danielson, & Hallahan, 2002). In their book, *Diagnosing Learning Disabilities*, Bush and Waugh (1976) defined a learning disability as "a disturbance in the perceptual, conceptual, memory, and/or expressive processes of learning, interfering with the interchange of communication" (p. 4). These authors categorize learning disabilities as "being limited to the intellectually normal and intellectually bright and gifted" (p. 4). It was during this era that much controversy began over the nature of learning disabilities and how best to identify and educate children with the diagnosis.

Though the federal government acknowledged in Public Law 91-230 that learning disabilities were, in fact, a category of disabilities eligible for federal supplementary funding, individual states were left with the task of outlining how such a disability would be serviced in their particular state. Mercer, Forgnone, and Wolking (1976) conducted a survey with 42 state departments of education to determine which definitions were being used and how those definitions were being utilized in public education systems. The researchers found that over 57% of states were using the NACHC definition; however, much variability was noted among states as to how LD was identified. Moreover, with the passage of Public Law 94-142, the U.S. Office of Education was asked to outline more precisely the definition of LD (as cited in Mercer, Hughes, & Mercer, 1985). Specificity was not released until 1977 with the Federal Register, which included the use of an IQ–achievement discrepancy model to determine LD eligibility. Mercer and colleagues (1985) later pointed out that, "the discrepancy and exclusion factors are basic to defining LD, whereas the psychological process factor remains optional" (p. 46). (Interestingly, this perspective would change to include the psychological process factor in later years, as described below).

Commonality among definitions in past decades existed only in the idea that learning disabilities were intrinsic to the individual and that a discrepancy existed (National Joint Committee on Learning Disabilities, 1991). Due to conceptual uncertainty, the federal definition of learning disabilities in the 1980s included children who were not achieving commensurate with their potential but who were ineligible for special education services under a different label (Short, Feagans, McKinney, & Appelbaum, 1986). This meant that students who were struggling in schools and needed assistance provided only through special education services, but could not meet any other eligibility criteria defined by the federal regulations, were called "learning disabled" by exclusion, meaning that everything else was excluded so it must be LD. Obvious problems with this argument are noted.

Some researchers even went as far as dissecting the federal definition line-by-line in an effort to make sense of the ambiguity. Hammill, Leigh, McNutt, and Larsen (1988) took on the federal definition and in 1981 published a new definition for learning disabilities through the National Joint Committee for Learning Disabilities (NJCLD). The NJCLD "believed strongly that the definition had inherent weaknesses . . . [limiting] a field as broad and complex as that of learning disabilities" (Hammill et al., 1988, p. 109). This committee found the word "children" in Public Law 94-142 to be too restrictive and the phrase "basic psychological processes" to be too inclusive; differentiating between intrinsic learning disabilities and those caused by sociological factors was necessary (Hammill et al., 1988). Also to be considered was the list of conditions (minimal brain dysfunction, dyslexia, etc.) because these additions to the definition only add to the confusion. The exclusions provided in the federal definition were also addressed because the committee felt that mentioning those sociological factors in the way they were mentioned suggested that those factors could be secondary, rather than primary, causes for learning disabilities; the committee felt that those factors were irrelevant to the diagnosis of learning disabilities. Ultimately, the committee provided this definition:

> . . . a generic term . . . heterogeneous group of disorders manifested by significant difficulties in the acquisition and use of listening, speaking, reading, writing, reasoning or mathematical abilities . . . intrinsic to the individual and presumed to be due to central nervous system dysfunction . . . may occur concomitantly with other handicapping conditions or environmental influences [but] is not the direct result of those conditions or influences. (Hammill et al., 1988, pp. 220–221)

Essentially, this means that any child who is not acquiring the necessary subject matter is eligible for special education services as a child with a learning disability. Though one can surely appreciate how many hours it must have taken to dissect the federal definition word for word and create a new definition, this new definition essentially supports what McKinney (as cited in Hallahan & Mercer, 2002) noted in 1983: that learning disabilities are characterized by unexpected underachievement. In 1986, the Learning Disabilities Association of America (LDA) provided a definition that was different from others in that it included the lifelong nature of learning disabilities and a reference to adaptive behavior, but it lacks an exclusion clause:

> . . . a chronic condition of presumed neurological origin which selectively interferes with the development, integration, and/or demonstration of verbal and/or nonverbal abilities . . . a distinct handicapping condition and varies in its manifestations and . . . severity. . . . Throughout life, the condition can affect self-esteem, education, vocation, socialization, and/or daily living activities. (Hallahan & Mercer, 2002, p. 39)

The reauthorization of IDEA in 2004 as the Individuals with Disabilities Education Improvement Act (IDEIA) was marked by a number of changes in the definition or diagnosis of LD in public schools. Possibly as a result of the nagging and pushing by frustrated teachers, petulant researchers, insistent parents, and still underachieving students, new language was proposed as part of IDEIA. Though the exclusion clause has not been eliminated, regulations explain that states may not *require* that school districts use the discrepancy model as a means for identifying children with learning disabilities (U.S. Department of Education, 2005). In specifying that school districts could not be required to use any specific model, the power to determine LD eligibility was given to individual states and local school districts. IDEIA now allows "the use of alternative, research-based approaches in lieu of (or in addition to) the Response to Intervention and traditional ability-achievement discrepancy methods" (Flanagan, Fiorello, & Ortiz 2010, p. 741). More specifically, the language in the federal regulations indicates that the state:

(1) must not require the use of a severe discrepancy between intellectual ability and achievement for determining whether a child has a specific learning disability;
(2) must permit the use of a process based on the child's response to scientific, research-based intervention; and
(3) may permit the use of other alternative research-based procedures for determining whether a child has a specific learning disability. (34 C.F.R. 300.540–543)

Part 3 appears to be the crux of the matter as states and local education agencies can now make their own determinations about most appropriate methods for LD eligibility, provided that such methods are research-based. As will be shown through the case study details below, this "third method" approach allows for inconsistencies across schools, school districts, and cities and such inconsistencies are becoming increasingly problematic for students on the receiving end.

Identification Approaches

With the allowance for additional approaches to LD eligibility determination, local education agencies are left to decide eligibility criteria independently. In doing so, some districts initially adopted a model that used a modified discrepancy approach comparing actual achievement and predicted achievement based upon cognitive abilities profile, while others used a combination of ideas. The following discussion focuses on four commonly used approaches to learning disability identification, all of which are alternatives to the simple discrepancy approach. Though equally valid, each approach must be used by the evaluator within the context of the evaluation referral.

Four Questions Approach

At the time of the case described below, most school districts in Texas (where the case occurred) were adopting, at least partially, a guidance approach to LD eligibility determination developed by Cheramie (2009) using the following four questions:

1. Is there a normative deficit in academic achievement?
2. Is there a pattern of strengths and weaknesses within the cognitive profile?
3. Is there a link between cognitive weaknesses and academic deficits?
4. Is there a functional impairment?

Question one focuses only on the child's performance on standardized academic achievement tests; however, question two is a bit more complex. A pattern of strengths and weaknesses is determined when all seven broad areas of cognitive processing are assessed using standardized cognitive assessment tools, as suggested by the Cattell Horn Carroll (CHC) theory of intelligence (Keith & Reynolds, 2010). Unlike previous models that required only an overall global IQ score, the CHC model is based on the theory that overall intelligence cannot be described using a single IQ score; moreover, intelligence can only be understood when several areas of cognitive processing are assessed using multiple subtests.

Question three of Cheramie's model addresses whether there is a link between cognitive weaknesses and academic deficits, and this link is established through research-based modalities. Current ideas suggest that there is a definitive link between cognitive abilities in several domains and success in reading, both in decoding and comprehension. For example, deficits in fluid reasoning may create difficulties with drawing inferences from text and abstracting main ideas as is required in reading. Deficits in visual processing may cause difficulties in math when the child is required to interpret graphs, tables, and charts

(Flanagan, Ortiz, & Alfonso, 2013). Finally, question four allows the examiner to evaluate whether the cognitive deficits are manifesting themselves in the classroom or within the grade-level curriculum. These questions are answered once all evaluation data have been obtained, and although four "yes" responses are not required for LD eligibility to be established, this is generally how the questions are applied.

PSW Approach

Another method of determining LD eligibility focuses exclusively on the pattern of strengths and weaknesses (PSW), which involves the use of computer software. The PSW approach has emerged as empirically sound and is supported by several researchers in the field, most notably by Flanagan (e.g., Flanagan et al., 2013). This model requires a relationship between cognitive deficits and academic achievement weaknesses, meaning that evaluators must assess both cognitive abilities and academic achievement skills and then address whether deficits in one create deficits in the other; however, one of the hallmark pieces of this approach is the use of a computer software program that purports to assist evaluators with the determination of whether a specific learning disability exists by providing quantitative information.

To use this model, evaluators are required to administer cognitive battery subtests that assess different narrow abilities as they relate to the seven broad abilities. For example, within the crystallized intelligence broad ability, subtests are administered that assess two narrow abilities such as lexical knowledge and general verbal information. This is done through the use of two separate subtests that assess different narrow abilities for each broad ability domain, and subtests are chosen based upon the impact of those narrow abilities on the area of suspected academic difficulty. Those scores are then inputted into the XBA Data Management and Interpretive Assistant (DMIA) and the XBA Pattern of Strengths and Weaknesses Analyzer (PSW Analyzer) (Flanagan et al., 2013). By following a detailed set of instructions, the evaluator will be able to obtain what is known as a g-value. This g-value is a statistically manipulated piece of data that tells the evaluator "how likely it is that the assessed child's pattern of strengths indicates at least average overall cognitive ability, despite one or more specific cognitive weaknesses or deficits" (Flanagan et al., 2013, p. 462). According to the manual provided for the software program, the g-value "was created to answer this question: Is the individual's overall cognitive ability at least average when the cognitive deficit(s) is not included in the estimate?" (Flanagan et al., 2013, p. 459). According to the same manual for the program, a g-value is calculated based upon the evaluator's judgment of the meaningfulness of specific cognitive areas, not on the scores themselves. Moreover, if the evaluator determines that a broad ability score is not sufficient, that score will not be included in the calculation of the g-value, which would lead the computer program to indicate that clinical judgment is needed to proceed.

Luria Method

The Luria method of cognitive assessment is based on Luria's model of intelligence, which differs from the CHC organization of broad and narrow abilities. Luria suggested that intelligence can best be understood by focusing on mental processing while deemphasizing acquired knowledge, or crystallized intelligence, as this theory considers acquired knowledge to reside outside of innate cognitive processing (Kaufman & Kaufman, 2004). According to the examiner's manual for this cognitive battery, the Luria model is preferred for students "with known or suspected language disorders, whether expressive, receptive, or mixed receptive-expressive" (Kaufman & Kaufman, 2004, p. 5). In addition, a hallmark difference between CHC theory and the Luria model exists: specific cognitive abilities are central to CHC theory, while the Luria model approaches cognitive assessment through a problem-solving, overall processing lens.

Response to Intervention (RTI)

RTI, though not specifically defined and only loosely applied, involves the use of evidence-based interventions with children who are struggling prior to referring these children for evaluation. Presumably, if the child responds well to these interventions, then the child is not referred for a psychoeducational evaluation to determine the presence of a disability; in contrast, a lack of response or minimal progress would warrant an evaluation for learning disability. Such an approach appears to be multifaceted, but it leaves much room for subjectivity, specifically with the use of interventions and a child's progress with or failure to respond to those interventions. Research supports the use of interventions in the classroom at varying levels to assist with academic difficulties for struggling students (e.g., Fuchs & Vaughn, 2012). However, the use of interventions and subsequent progress monitoring systems in schools varies in the delivery models, which leads to inconsistencies among local education agencies (e.g., Fletcher & Vaughn, 2009).

CASE STUDY

Charles was a student who had previously been identified with a speech and language impairment, specifically severe phonology issues and a receptive and expressive language disorder, while in kindergarten in a large urban public school district in Texas (District A). He had been receiving speech and language therapy in the school setting and the home setting consistently since that time. He was retained in kindergarten and moved to District B for his second year of kindergarten, after which he was promoted to first grade. While in first grade, Charles continued to struggle in reading, and classroom interventions were provided. According to records, these interventions included small group instruction, individualized attention, checks for understanding, repeated review, and drill and repetition of sight words. He was promoted to second grade but continued to struggle in reading. In addition, Charles began having difficulties in math as well.

Interventions provided in first grade were continued in second grade, and the following intervention programs were added to his repertoire: Guided Reading, Earobics, Accelerated Reading, DI Reading, FASST Math, and En Vision Computerized Math. Though Charles showed improvements using these programs, his rate of improvement was quite poor. He was not performing as expected for a child his age in reading or math, and data show that during the middle part of second grade Charles was reading at a level of K.4 (kindergarten fourth month) and that his math skills were at a level of 1.1 (first grade first month). Due to continued academic difficulties, Charles was referred for a full psychoeducational evaluation in second grade (2009-10 school year) to determine the presence of a learning disability.

Evaluation #1

A review of the psychoeducational report that was written indicates that the Woodcock Johnson III Tests of Cognitive Abilities (WJIII COG; Schrank, McGrew, & Mather, 2014b) was administered for that 2010 evaluation (second grade), and the following standard scores were reported: Crystallized Intelligence – 78, Fluid Reasoning – 78, Long Term Retrieval – 69, Processing Speed – 85, Short-Term Memory – 79, Visual Spatial Thinking – 112, and Auditory Processing – 88. Though Charles's overall cognitive ability standard score was reported to be low (General Intellectual Ability – 77), it was noted that this score "[should have been] interpreted with caution as there [was] significant variability both within and between the cognitive processing clusters" (Full and Individual Evaluation, 2010, p. 6). In addition, the impact of his poor language development and continued difficulties with a receptive and expressive language disorder could not be ruled out as a causative factor for poor performance on the subtests that make up the crystallized intelligence cluster standard score.

Charles was also administered the Woodcock Johnson III Tests of Achievement (WJIII ACH; Schrank, McGrew, & Mather, 2014a), and the following standard scores were reported: Basic Reading Skills – 63, Reading Comprehension – 75, Brief Reading – 61, Math Calculation Skills – 89, Math Reasoning – 80, Broad Math – 89, Brief Writing Skills – 75, and Written Expression – 72. A dyslexia evaluation was completed as well, and it was determined that Charles was a student with a learning disability in basic reading skills and with dyslexia (the latter of which, strangely, is not considered a learning disability in Texas). Eligibility was determined by identifying the presence of cognitive weaknesses that negatively impacted academic skills combined with a failure to respond to interventions appropriately.

At the time of Charles's initial psychoeducational evaluation, District B was using Cheramie's (2009) four question approach to LD eligibility determination. In order to respond to the first question, the evaluator must review the data obtained from the standardized academic achievement battery(s) administered. The response in Charles's case was affirmative in that he displayed significant academic weaknesses as measured by the WJIII ACH in Basic Reading Skills, Reading Comprehension, Math Reasoning, and Written Expression.

In response to the second question, "Is there a pattern of cognitive strengths and weaknesses?" the response was again "yes." As indicated by his performance on the WJIII COG, Charles displayed average abilities in processing speed, visual spatial thinking, and auditory processing. The FIE report indicates that his abilities in crystallized intelligence were suspect because they appeared to be attenuated by poor language skills, meaning that skills in this cognitive domain could not be determined. True cognitive deficits were noted in fluid reasoning, long-term retrieval, and short-term memory. Interestingly enough, Flanagan (2007) may have responded differently to the second question, suggesting that Charles displayed the pattern of a child with pervasive difficulties rather than specific cognitive deficits. Flanagan may have indicated that Charles was a slow learner because he performed below what is expected for a child his age in three out of seven broad ability domains. (A fourth domain, crystallized intelligence, also shows low abilities, though one would need to discount the impact of poor language development in order to identify this domain as weak with any certainty.) According to Flanagan (2013), this pattern is inconsistent with the LD construct because LD is based on "the notion that individuals with specific learning disabilities are of generally average or better overall cognitive ability" (p. 266).

Question three of Cheramie's model addresses whether there is a link between cognitive deficiencies and academic deficits. Charles demonstrated significant cognitive weaknesses in fluid reasoning, comprehension knowledge, long-term retrieval, and short term memory. Though specific difficulties in academic skills were not noted, definitive links between Charles's cognitive weaknesses and academic achievement difficulties in reading were determined, and this resulted in a response of "yes" to question three.

The final question that is addressed as part of this model and was used in District B deals with the notion of a functional impairment that manifests itself in the form of poor classroom performance. Here, the numerous interventions and intervention programs that were used coupled with failing grades and a history of academic difficulties led to a response of yes to this question. This pattern of affirmatives led to Charles receiving LD eligibility in basic reading skills in District B.

Evaluation #2

In fourth grade (2011–12 school year), Charles moved back to District A, where he continued to receive dyslexia services along with special education supports. When he transferred back to District A, all services and supports mirrored those of the previous district, as is mandated by IDEIA. In addition, the 2010 evaluation report was reviewed by campus staff and accepted so that Charles's eligibility as a child with a learning disability was continued without any additional evaluation. This means that the receiving school (District A) reviewed the evaluation report completed by the sending school (District B) and determined that the evaluation was completed in ways similar and acceptable to the methods in which evaluations are completed in the receiving district.

In fifth grade (2012–13), Charles transferred to District C, where he continued to receive special education services as a student with a learning disability in basic reading skills. The transfer process was the same in that the 2010 evaluation completed in District B was reviewed and accepted by the new school in District C. However, once Charles reached seventh grade in District C (winter of 2014), he was required to undergo reevaluation. The evaluation staff administered the WJIII COG, and the following standard scores were reported: Crystallized Intelligence – 77, Long Term Retrieval – 70, Visual Processing – 96, Auditory Processing – 88, Fluid Reasoning – 87, Processing Speed – 96, and Short Term Memory – 81. Charles's General Intellectual Ability (GIA) standard score was in the Low Average range (standard score – 81). He was also administered select subtests from the WJIII ACH, and the following standard scores were reported: Letter Word Identification – 79, Word Attack – 84, Basic Reading Skills – 80, Passage Comprehension – 76, Reading Vocabulary – 79, and Reading Comprehension – 76. Because he had previously been diagnosed with a learning disability in Basic Reading Skills, the Gray Oral Reading Tests – Fifth Edition (GORT – 5) was also administered as part of that reevaluation, and his Oral Reading Index standard score was 70 (two standard deviations below the mean). No formal assessment was completed in Math or Writing as part of that same reevaluation.

Interestingly enough, the 2014 evaluation team (District C) used the same four question approach (Cheramie, 2009) that District B had used to identify Charles as having a specific learning disability. However,

District C determined that Charles did not meet eligibility for services as a student with a learning disability, even though the pattern of data was remarkably similar to the data obtained by District B several years earlier. Instead, the 2014 evaluation report indicates that Charles was better described as a child with general learning difficulties, or a slow learner.

District C's decision was influenced by the PSW approach, which attempts to address Cheramie's (2009) second question with greater precision and accuracy. Using Charles's standard scores on the WJIII, the evaluator entered the information into the computer software program (DMIA and PSW Analyzer) and a g-value of 0.38 was obtained. According to the program, this means that Charles's overall cognitive ability was unlikely to be average. This conclusion stems from initial entries into the software program that indicate whether the standard scores obtained in each of the seven broad ability areas is "sufficient" (i.e., contributes meaningfully to Charles's overall intellectual functioning). A standard score is deemed "sufficient" by the evaluator, and a determination of "sufficiency" is typically made for standard scores that are approximately 90 (in the average range) or above.

However, it cannot be ignored that there are "many variables [that] facilitate or inhibit an individual's performance on psychological tests. . . [and] evaluators [may] use clinical judgment when determining whether the abilities are sufficient" (Flanagan et al., 2013, p. 462). Here lies part of the issue at hand: The computer software program is only as accurate as the person who is inputting the information and thereby dictating to the computer program whether scores should or should not be included in the calculation of the g-value. If the information entered is a result of the clinical judgment and interpretation from the evaluator, one would naturally assume the conclusion rendered is subjective as well. In Charles's case, this is precisely what happened.

The evaluator in Charles's case in District C entered all cognitive scores into the software program but did not use 90 as the cutoff score for determining whether a standard score was sufficient; instead, the evaluator used clinical judgment to determine that any standard scores more than one standard deviation below the mean (below 85) were not sufficient (crystallized intelligence, long-term retrieval, short-term memory), which led to the g-value of 0.38. The evaluator in this case determined that Charles no longer met eligibility for special education services as a student with a learning disability because the g-value led the evaluator to respond "no" to question two: Charles did *not* display a pattern of cognitive strengths and weaknesses. Because the evaluator determined that Charles was instead a slow learner, question three was not addressed, as academic deficits are to be expected for a child with pervasive cognitive difficulties. No weight was placed on other data sources and question four was not answered, as indicated in the summary of the evaluation report. Furthermore, no credence was given to Charles's diagnosed expressive and receptive language disorder as an attenuating factor in the calculation of his crystallized intelligence standard score.

Evaluation #3

Charles's parent was in disagreement with the discontinuance of the LD eligibility and requested an independent educational evaluation to be completed at the district's expense. This evaluation was completed by a doctoral-level educational diagnostician approximately three months later. As part of the independent evaluation, multiple data sources were used to determine the presence of a learning disability including parent interviews, review of records, classroom observations, and formal assessment. However, formal assessment was completed differently by the independent evaluator.

Because Charles had a history of speech and language issues, the Luria model of the Kaufman Assessment Battery for Children–Second Edition (KABC II; Kaufman & Kaufman, 2004) was used to determine cognitive processing abilities. This model was chosen as part of the method for determining current levels of cognitive processing and the following standard scores were reported (comparable CHC language is provided in parentheses): Sequential Reasoning (Short-Term Memory) – 77, Simultaneous Reasoning (Visual Spatial Thinking) – 112, Learning (Long-Term Retrieval) – 84, and Planning (Fluid Reasoning) – 99. Auditory Processing skills were assessed using the Comprehensive Test of Phonological Processing – Second Edition (CTOPP2; Wagner, Torgesen, Rashotte, & Pearson, 2013). This was reportedly done for two purposes. First, a comprehensive assessment of auditory processing skills was completed using an entire battery of tests rather than two subtests of narrow abilities related to auditory processing. Second, Charles had a history of dyslexia and the CTOPP2 is widely used to determine the presence of this disorder. In contrast to previous evaluation results that showed average auditory processing, Charles displayed significant weaknesses in all areas of auditory processing as indicated by the following standard scores: Phonological Awareness – 73, Phonological Memory – 64, and Rapid Naming – 64. Processing speed was not assessed by the independent evaluator.

Charles was also administered the Kaufman Test of Educational Achievement – Third Edition (KTEA 3; Kaufman & Kaufman, 2015) and the following standard scores were reported: Reading – 73, Math – 79, and Written Language – 77. More specifically, Charles displayed below grade level skills in all areas of reading. He could decode text at levels similar to a child in second grade (standard score – 67), and his fluency skills were below age expectations as well (standard score – 84). He could not comprehend what he read independently (standard score – 80), and his reading vocabulary skills were poor (standard score – 76). In math, Charles had similar difficulties. He appeared to lack the automaticity of math facts that was expected for a child his age (standard score – 83), and his computation skills and problem solving skills were equally poor (standard scores – 78 and 83, respectively). Written expression skills were at age-appropriate levels, but Charles's spelling and writing fluency were very poorly developed.

The independent evaluator used a different approach to determine that Charles *did* display the profile of a child with a learning disability in basic reading skills. This evaluator did not use the PSW analyzer, as this would have been inappropriate because that computer software is built upon CHC theory and requires the assessment of all seven broad abilities. In Charles's case, all seven abilities were not assessed; both processing speed and crystallized intelligence were not formally evaluated, though no explanation was provided for the lack of assessment of Charles's processing speed abilities.

The approach used by the independent evaluator would also be considered a "third method" approach as permitted in part three of the federal regulations; the approach is similar to the approaches used in the two previous evaluations. Cheramie's four questions were used to help guide the decision-making process, and multiple data sources were relied upon to continue the LD eligibility in basic reading skills.

In response to question one, the independent evaluator indicated obvious academic difficulties in basic reading skills, reading comprehension, math calculation, and math reasoning. With regard to question two, the independent evaluator responded with "yes" and listed then-current and previous evaluation data to determine that a pattern of strengths and weaknesses *did* exist. Of the five cognitive abilities assessed, Charles was weak in three: auditory processing, short-term memory, and long-term retrieval. Using Flanagan's model (Flanagan, Ortiz, & Alfonso, 2007), the independent evaluator noted that three weaknesses out of five assessed cognitive processing domains may suggest the profile of a slow learner; however, Charles had a previous diagnosis of dyslexia and severe phonology issues, which were used to explain his poor performance on the auditory processing subtests.

In addition, the independent evaluator acknowledged the previous evaluations of Charles's cognitive processing skills and suggested that Charles's language issues were consistently problematic. Though processing speed was not assessed as part of the independent evaluation, those skills were noted in the summary report—Charles had demonstrated intact processing speed abilities in both the 2010 and 2014 psychoeducational evaluations, suggesting no deficits in this domain. By removing crystallized intelligence from the equation, the independent evaluator was able to establish overall average ability over the course of the previous four years using all three evaluation data points. This allowed the evaluator to respond with "yes" to question two: there was a pattern of cognitive strengths and weaknesses, provided that poor language skills were identified as a causative factor in Charles's performances on subtests in the crystallized intelligence domain. Furthermore, auditory processing skills were historically age appropriate. Charles's poor performance on the CTOPP2 was likely a result of phonology issues and dyslexia rather than innate cognitive processing deficits, and it was noted that the CTOPP2 was a much more comprehensive assessment of skills in this domain than had been completed in previous evaluations.

The independent evaluator also cited the consistent pattern over time, indicating that Charles had displayed cognitive weaknesses in short-term memory and long-term retrieval on all three psychoeducational evaluations. All of the cognitive data, both historical and current, were used to respond to question three with "yes," as links could be established among Charles's difficulties in crystallized knowledge, short-term memory, and long-term retrieval. It was noted in the report that while crystallized intelligence was attenuated by poor language skills, this domain still impacted Charles academically, as schools are verbal, language-loaded institutions. That being said, weaknesses in crystallized intelligence were cited as causing struggles with vocabulary development and with knowledge acquisition, in addition to poor understanding of the nuances of language. Because he may have had difficulty finding the right words to use or say, it was anticipated that Charles could have a hard time answering fact-based/informational questions, and he would struggle to use prior knowledge to support new learning.

Deficits in long-term retrieval could cause Charles to have difficulties learning new concepts as he tries to retrieve or recall information by using association, and it was anticipated that he would have a difficult time with rapid retrieval of information and with generating ideas quickly. As a result of short-term memory issues, the evaluator noted that Charles may struggle to recall sequences and memorize factual information, and he may find it difficult to follow multi-step instructions or maintain his place in a math problem. He could also struggle to reason through math problems, as he may not always remember all of the steps involved or all of the details embedded within the problem itself. The following statement was also provided in response to question three: "It is important to note that, according to the examiner's manual for the CTOPP–2, students who have deficits in both rapid naming and phonological awareness are at greater risk of reading problems than students who have deficits in only one of those two areas" (Full and Individual Evaluation, 2015, p. 14).

Question four, which addressed the functional impairment that may be the manifestation of the cognitive and academic weaknesses in the classroom, was answered by providing significant details about Charles's classroom performance. The explanation for this response included Charles's grades and performance on state-mandated assessments along with the acknowledgment of special education supports and services that Charles had been requiring in order to meet grade level standards. Additionally, the independent evaluator cited a guidance document that the Texas Education Agency (TEA) developed after IDEIA authorization to address students who were previously identified as having a learning disability but who did not meet the new identification criteria. The guidance document (TEA, n.d.) indicates that, when conducting a special education re-evaluation for LD eligibility, schools are encouraged to:

1) use caution in determining that a child is no longer eligible for special education services;

2) carefully consider the child's response to removal of such supports; and
3) examine whether the special education instruction has been appropriate and, if so, whether such evidence argues for a continuation of LD eligibility. (pp. 2–3)

In addition, "A major consideration in the reevaluation process should be the student's ability to meet the instructional demands of grade-level standards without special education and related services" (Texas Education Agency, n.d., p. 3). The independent evaluator determined that Charles would have significant difficulty progressing in the general education curriculum if the special education services he had been receiving were removed.

Though the independent evaluator concluded that Charles did, in fact, meet eligibility criteria for special education services as a child with a learning disability, the school district did not agree. The independent evaluation was initially rejected by the school district, despite protests from Charles's parent. The school district noted that, while the independent evaluator used an empirically-based and psychometrically sound model, that model was not the one adopted by that particular school district. In disagreement, the parent requested that the school district communicate directly with the independent evaluator for further explanation of the findings of the new evaluation (as Charles's parent obviously thought that Charles *did* have a learning disability). This conversation between the school district and the independent evaluator led to the district's acceptance of the independent evaluation. Ultimately, Charles's LD eligibility was restored.

DISCUSSION AND RECOMMENDATIONS

Charles's case is not exceptional in any regard, and students are finding themselves caught in the crossfire between local education agencies when LD determinations are made. The inconsistencies stem directly from the power given to schools and school districts to determine their own methods of LD diagnosis. The "third method" approach is meant to allow schools the option of using research-based methods in eligibility decisions, but because no standard has been set for this "third method," schools are left to make those decisions themselves.

Additionally, it cannot be ignored that the discrepancy model was much cleaner and easier for practitioners to understand. This is not to endorse that model, as it was inherently flawed; however, the discrepancy model left almost nothing in the gray areas like those of the third method approaches being used. Cross-battery assessment requires massive amounts of training and manpower, along with continuous opportunities for growth. It is no easy task to complete a full psychoeducational assessment for a child suspected of having a learning disability, and rightfully so, but having such a system requires that schools and school districts operate in similar fashion. Students should not be able to change eligibilities simply because they moved schools.

In Charles's case, his initial evaluation was completed in District B and was later accepted by school staff in District C. He changed schools, remaining in District C, and when a reevaluation was completed, the new school staff concluded that he was not a child with a learning disability simply because their model for determination had changed. This is severely flawed and begs the question about the LD construct itself: Is it real, and if so, how can it be so relative to context? How can its existence be subject to the interpretation, or clinical judgment, of an evaluator who may or may not have had training in new approaches or whose clinical judgment differs from other evaluators?

Most school districts in Texas have adopted Cheramie's four question approach to LD eligibility, and answering "yes" to all four questions typically suggests the presence of a learning disability. Adoption of the PSW approach, along with the computer software, is being done to varying degrees across school districts nationwide, with at least 15 states reporting use of the PSW approach to identification (Coomer, 2015). Some districts are "all in" and use the computer software as the diagnostician instead of simply as a tool to assist with data obtained. Other districts are not using the computer software at all and are simply addressing unexpected underachievement, however that is defined. While this may be infinitely better than in decades past for determining eligibility for special education services, evaluators are still working with a political and social construct that is used in the provision or denial of a free and appropriate education. Not only is there disagreement about what a learning disability is, but the methods of determining its existence differ to such a great degree that a child can literally have a learning disability in one school and be ineligible for such services in another school. This is absurd; if LD really exists and if schools are really going to teach all children, practitioners nationwide must come to some agreement about what LD is and how it is going to be identified so that appropriate instructional programs for these students can be provided.

In contrast to the current methods of evaluation, an alternative approach would likely garner more useful information and yield more effective recommendations. Rather than idolizing one specific approach to the identification of learning disabilities (as they are all flawed in some fashion), practitioners should be empowered to identify individual needs for each student. Consistency in identification models should come in the form of identifying what a child needs and providing exactly that. Such an approach would begin with identifying the child's background and experiences. It would then focus on determining what the child's interests are and at what the child excels. It would also involve exploring what a child's challenge areas are. Once such information were obtained, school personnel would meet as a team not to determine *whether* the child gets what he or she needs but *how* to provide what the child needs. Those needs could include structured learning classrooms, parent/home intervention training, and teacher training and staff development. Recommendations could involve anything from direct one-to-one instruction to enrichment programs that specifically target identified savant qualities that the child possesses.

It is time to re-evaluate the evaluation procedures and the ways in which eligibility decisions are made. Until common sense and consistency guide the identification of LDs, students like Charles will continue to be vulnerable to idiosyncrasies in how states and districts interpret special education law.

REFERENCES

Algozzine, B., & Ysseldkye, J. E. (1987). Questioning discrepancies: Retaking the first step 20 years later. *Learning Disability Quarterly, 10*(4), 201–312.

Bradley, R., Johnson, M. K., Danielson, L. C., & Hallahan, D. P. (2002). *Identification of learning disabilities: Research to practice.* New York: Routledge.

Bush, W. J., & Waugh, K. W. (1976). *Diagnosing learning disabilities.* Columbus, Ohio: Charles E. Merrill.

Cheramie, G. (2009, June). Identification of learning disabilities. Presentation at Education Service Center Region 4, Houston, TX.

Coomer, L. F. (2015). Definitions and criteria used by state education departments for identifying specific learning disabilities (Unpublished specialist project). Western Kentucky University, Bowling Green, KY.

Education of the Handicapped Act of 1970, Pub. L. No. 91-230, 84 Stat. 121 (1970).

Flanagan, D., Fiorello, C., & Ortiz, S. (2010). Enhancing practice through application of Catell-Horn-Carroll theory and research: A "third method" approach to specific learning disability identification. *Psychology in the Schools, 47*(7), 739–760.

Flanagan, D., Ortiz, S., & Alfonso, V. (2007). *Essentials of cross-battery assessment* (2nd ed.). Hoboken, NJ: John Wiley & Sons.

Flanagan, D., Ortiz, S., & Alfonso, V. (2013). *Essentials of cross-battery assessment* (3rd ed.). Hoboken, NJ: John Wiley & Sons.

Fletcher, J. M., & Vaughn, S. (2009). Response to intervention: Preventing and remediating academic difficulties. *Child Development Perspectives, 3*(1), 30–37.

Fuchs, L. S., & Vaughn, S. (2012). Responsiveness-to-Intervention: A decade later. *Journal of Learning Disabilities, 45*(3), 195–203.

Full and Individual Evaluation. (2010). [Additional source information has been omitted to preserve the student's anonymity.]

Hallahan, D. P., & Mercer, C. D. (2002). Learning disabilities: Historical perspectives. In R. Bradley, L. Danielson, & D. P. Hallahan (Eds.), *Identification of learning disabilities: Research to practice* (pp. 1–67). Mahwah, NJ: Lawrence Erlbaum.

Hammill, D. D., Leigh, J. E., McNutt, G., & Larsen, S. (1988). A new definition of learning disabilities. *Learning Disability Quarterly, 11*(3), 217–223.

Kaufman, A. S., & Kaufman, N. L. (2004). *Kaufman Assessment Battery for Children* (2nd ed.). Circle Pines, MN: American Guidance Service.

Kaufman, A. S., & Kaufman, N. L. (2015). *Kaufman Test of Educational Achievement* (3rd ed.). Circle Pines, MN: American Guidance Service.

Keith, T. Z., & Reynolds, M. R. (2010). Cattell-Horn-Carroll abilities and cognitive tests: What we've learned from 20 years of research. *Psychology in the Schools, 47*(7), 635-650.

Kirk, S. A. (1972). *Educating exceptional children.* Boston: Houghton-Mifflin.

Learning Disabilities: Issues on Definition. (1990, January). Retrieved October 27, 2007, from National Center for Learning Disabilities: http://www.ncld.org/content/view/458/

Mercer, C. D., Forgnone, C., & Wolking, W. D. (1976). Definitions of learning disabilities used in the United States. *Journal of Learning Disabilities, 9*, 376–386.

Mercer, C. D., Hughes, C., & Mercer, A. R. (1985). Learning disabilities definitions used by state education departments. *Learning Disability Quarterly, 8*(1), 45-55.

McCormick, S. (1995). *Instructing students who have literacy problems.* Englewood Cliffs, NJ: Prentice-Hall.

National Joint Committee on Learning Disabilities. (1991). Learning disabilities: Issues on definition. *Asha, 33*, (Suppl. 5), 18–20.

Schrank, F. A., McGrew, K. S., & Mather, N. (2014a). *Woodcock-Johnson IV Tests of Achievement.* Rolling Meadows, IL: Riverside.

Schrank, F. A., McGrew, K. S., & Mather, N. (2014b). *Woodcock-Johnson IV Tests of Cognitive Abilities.* Rolling Meadows, IL: Riverside.

Short, E. J., Feagans, L., McKinney, J. D., & Appelbaum, M. I. (1986). Longitudinal stability of LD subtypes based on age- and IQ–achievement discrepancies. *Learning Disability Quarterly, 9*(3), 214–225.

Swanson, H. L., Graham, S., & Harris, K. R. (2005). *Handbook of learning disabilities.* Guilford Press.

Texas Education Agency. (n.d.) Response to intervention and learning disability eligibility. Retrieved from http://www.txasp.org/assets/evaluation%20of%20learning%20disability%20eligibility.pdf

U.S. Department of Education, Office of Special Education and Rehabilitative Services, Office of Special Education Programs. (2003). *25th annual report to Congress on the implementation of the Individuals with Disabilities Education Act, vol. 1,* Washington, D.C., 2005. Retrieved from http://www.ed.gov/about/reports/annual/osep/2003/25th-vol-1-front.pdf

Wagner, R. K., Torgesen, J. K., Rashotte, C. A., & Pearson, N. A. (2013). *Comprehensive Test of Phonological Processing* (2nd ed). Austin, TX: PRO-ED.

Chapter 2

THE PLIGHT OF THE SLOW LEARNER

Tera Torres

INTRODUCTION

A specific learning disability (SLD) is defined by the Individuals with Disabilities Education Improvement Act of 2004 (IDEIA) as "a disorder in one or more of the basic psychological processes involved in understanding or using language . . . which manifests itself in the imperfect ability to listen, think, speak, read, write, spell, or do mathematical calculations. . ." (34 C.F.R. 300.8). In determining whether a child possesses such a disorder, federal regulations permit the use of several methods for this purpose and, as noted in the previous chapter, school districts in Texas and in many other states have adopted the pattern of strengths and weaknesses (PSW) approach to determining SLD eligibility (Coomer, 2015).

The learning disability construct is based on the notion that a child with such a disorder is an otherwise capable and intelligent student. In fact, the common thread among all models of determining the presence of a learning disability is *unexpected* underachievement; that is, a child who functions in the average range of cognitive abilities who does not perform academically at levels commensurate with his measured IQ may have a learning disability. Conversely, a child who is slow learning will not perform academically at average levels, regardless of whether instructional accommodations or curricular modifications are put into place. Such a child will inevitably struggle with whatever is presented, and school tends to be a place of extraordinary difficulty for these children. This is where the system is fundamentally flawed: Why do schools remediate the "bright" ones and leave the others to continue failing, falling through the proverbial cracks in the system? And why are we surprised when these students who are left to their own devices end up as nonreading adults or otherwise nonproductive citizens?

BACKGROUND

Historically, intellectual disability (formerly known as mental retardation) has been defined, at least in part, as having a measured cognitive ability score of more than two standard deviations below the mean. Using 100 as the mean of standard scores along with a standard deviation of 15, this means that the accepted score for intellectual disability has been one below 70. Furthermore, federal regulations allow for special education services to be provided to students who function in this range of abilities.

What federal legislation has not addressed in the past or currently is the student who falls just above that range of intellectual disability— what is known as Borderline Intellectual Functioning in the clinical realm. According to Wieland and Zitman (2016), this classification has been used in psychiatric settings since the earliest edition of the Diagnostic and Statistical Manual (DSM). These students function with cognitive ability scores measured to be between about 70 and 85 (between one and two standard deviations below the mean of standard scores). In schools, we call these same children "slow learners" and provide no special education classification or category under which they may receive special education programming. Moreover, a literature review conducted by Peltopuro, Ahonen, Kaartinen, Seppala, and Narhi (2014) indicates that special education services for these students has not been federally funded since at least 1973, when the distinction was made between students with intellectual disabilities (at the time labeled mental retardation) and students with specific learning disabilities.

Research on slow learners is somewhat limited, given that this group is not an identified population within special education law. In fact, according to Peltopuro et al. (2014), ". . . borderline intellectual functioning is a rarely studied topic . . . despite the high percentage of people in this category" (p. 419). However, some studies shed light on slow learners' current educational outcomes. Kaznowski (2004) studied more than 640 students in grades third through fifth, most of whom were identified as having learning disabilities and others who were identified as being "non-special education" (NSE), meaning that they did not qualify for services due to having a measured global cognitive ability level between 70 and 85. While this study did not explicitly address the plight of the slow learner, results of the study reveal that the students who received special education supports (those identified as LD) had higher high school grade point averages and earned more high school credits than the students who were identified as slow learners and were not provided with special education supports. In addition, results obtained suggested that slow learners "are not succeeding in school . . . barely earning passing grades, frequently credit deficient, scoring in the below average range on achievement tests . . . and not passing the proficiency exams" (Kaznowski, 2004, p. 40). According to Shaw (2010), these students are "dropping out of school, retained . . . are underemployed or unemployed" (p. 13), along with having a host of social and economic hardships.

CASE STUDY

Karla was seven-year-old Hispanic first-grader at an elementary school in a small urban school district during the 2014–2015 school year. The school itself serves approximately 600 students in grades pre-kindergarten though fifth and the student-teacher ratio for first grade classrooms was approximately 17:1 in 2014 (TEA School Report Card, 2014). Though the school is not specifically designated as a Title I funded school, approximately 81% of students were identified as economically disadvantaged that school year.

Karla reportedly struggled with academic tasks in kindergarten at this particular school, and she did not meet the school district's standards on any math assessments administered that year. At the end of the year in kindergarten, her skills in Math and Language Arts were rated by her teacher as "Still Developing." The Developmental Reading Assessment (DRA; Pearson, 2009), which is designed to identify a student's independent reading level including phonological awareness, phonics skills, accuracy, fluency, and comprehension, was also administered at the end of that school year. Karla's skills were determined to be significantly below grade level. She was nonetheless was placed in first grade and during the second semester of that first grade year, a dyslexia evaluation was completed to determine whether Karla's academic struggles were due to this disorder. As no such eligibility was determined, Karla was referred three months later to the special education department for a psychoeducational evaluation to determine the presence of a learning disability that would warrant special education services. It is important to note that, at least in Texas, dyslexia is not funded through special education programming.

At the conclusion of a psychoeducational evaluation, a report is generated, and this report is typically called the Full and Individual Evaluation (FIE). Best practices in the field require that this report reflect the entire assessment process and that all data sources be included in the determination of the presence of a disability. Thus, several key pieces of data are included in the report. With respect to psychoeducational evaluations for learning disability diagnosis, a reason for the referral must be noted along with sociological data that includes an educational history and parent interviews. Classroom observations must also be conducted in the instructional setting where the child appears to be struggling, and language proficiency must be addressed. A hearing and vision screening along with information about the child's health history must also be included, prior to any standardized assessment. Once all of those pieces are collected, an evaluator should conduct a comprehensive academic achievement assessment and full cognitive battery.

In Karla's case, all of this was completed. The hearing and vision screening indicated that Karla's hearing and vision were adequate for standardized assessment purposes, and Karla's parent reported no significant health history; however, Karla's parent did report a history of familial learning problems. Karla's father and uncle were diagnosed with learning disabilities at a young age, and Karla reportedly met developmental milestones at later ages than other family members.

A review of school records showed that Karla had been having significant difficulties throughout her almost-two years in school. Teachers reported that Karla was sometimes discouraged by difficulties and minor setbacks, and she did not always complete tasks independently. Her teachers rated Karla's ability to comprehend word meanings and her immediate auditory recall as "poor." She was rated "below average" by her teachers in her ability to follow oral directions and comprehend classroom discussions. She struggled to organize and relate ideas and factual information and was not able to relate a sequence of events in order. She was also rated "poor" on her task completion time and retention of instruction.

Academically, Karla's teachers reported that she did not display age-appropriate reading skills, nor could she read grade-level, high frequency words. She also could not decode multisyllabic grade-level words and was inconsistent in her ability to answer questions about the main idea of passages she read. Inferencing skills were also reportedly weak, as was her ability to summarize a short story that was read to her or that she read independently. Writing skills were exceedingly weak, as Karla was unable to write a simple sentence or a coherent paragraph that was appropriate for her age and grade. It was further reported that during the second semester of first grade, Karla's reading skills were measured to be at a level of K.2 (kindergarten, second month). Karla reportedly displayed equally problematic skills in math; she could not add and subtract at age appropriate levels and she could not solve grade-level word problems. Teacher-reported grades were very low that school year: Karla was consistently given failing grades in math, reading, and language arts.

Standardized academic achievement assessment was completed using the Woodcock Johnson Tests of Achievement – Fourth Edition (Schrank, McGrew, & Mather, 2014a), and the following standard scores were reported (mean = 100, standard deviation = 15): Basic Reading Skills – 64, Reading Comprehension – 57, Written Expression – 71, Math Calculation Skills – 81, and Math Problem Solving – 66. More specifically, the evaluator noted that Karla was able to identify individual letters but had limited skills in sight word recognition; Karla would apply phonetic skills in an apparent attempt to "sound out" words that students her age are expected to know and recognize automatically. She also struggled with the phonetic coding that is involved in sounding out unknown words. With respect to reading comprehension, Karla was able to match pictures to words that described the pictures but she was not able to consistently read one or two word phrases. She also could not read enough words in a given passage to facilitate comprehension of what was read.

Karla was able to write her first name but not her last name, and she appeared to use phonetic-type spelling to write words that children her age are expected to know how to spell. In Math, Karla used her fingers to add and subtract, which is developmentally appropriate; however, this made it impossible for her to add or subtract beyond the point at which she had fingers to show. She also struggled to solve one-step word problems involving addition and subtraction, and counting pennies and nickels was challenging for her. Karla's performance on the standardized academic achievement assessment was quite similar to her classroom performance, which is a point that is often overlooked in evaluations.

To assess Karla's cognitive abilities, the Kaufman Assessment Battery for Children – Second Edition (Kaufman & Kaufman, 2004) was administered, and the following standard scores were reported (mean = 100, standard deviation = 15): Comprehension Knowledge (Crystallized Intelligence) – 72, Long-Term Retrieval – 70, Fluid Reasoning – 93, Short Term Memory – 66, and Visual Processing – 81. Selected subtests from the Woodcock Johnson Tests of Cognitive Abilities – Fourth Edition (Schrank et al., 2014b) were also administered, and the following standard scores were reported (mean = 100, standard deviation = 15): Cognitive Processing Speed – 85 and Auditory Processing – 87. It is important to note here that Karla appeared to have significant cognitive deficits in several assessed domains. First, her crystallized intelligence skills were measured to be very weak, as indicated by her overall standard score of 72 in this area; she demonstrated poor knowledge base, or "general fund of knowledge," as it is commonly called. Both her short-term and long-term memory skills were also deemed highly inadequate along with her ability to process visual patterns and images. Interestingly, Karla's fluid reasoning skills were similar to same-age peers, and her ability to process information quickly was adequate (her standard score of 85 is within one standard deviation of the mean). Auditory Processing skills were age-appropriate, which indicated that her ability to analyze and make sense of auditory information was intact.

Karla displayed normative cognitive deficits in four out of seven assessed cognitive domains, and academic skills were weak across all subject areas. In applying the PSW approach to determine the presence of a learning disability, one would think that Karla possessed the necessary characteristics to meet eligibility criteria. After all, Karla did display cognitive weaknesses that could be directly linked as causative factors in her poor academic performance. Flanagan, Otiz, and Alfonso (2006) suggest that deficits in crystallized intelligence are likely to lead to difficulty with vocabulary acquisition and comprehending language, and Karla may have displayed problems accessing background knowledge to support new learning while reading. Significant weaknesses in memory have been linked to struggles with recall and retrieval and with remembering information long enough to apply it. Karla's deficits in long term memory may have caused her to have difficulty recalling information by using association strategies, and she may also have had difficulty following multistep directions as a result of demonstrated deficits in short-term memory skills. Visual processing difficulties often cause problems with recognizing patterns and reading graphic representations. Furthermore, orthographic coding difficulties along with sight word acquisition may also have been related to Karla's deficits in visual processing.

Shockingly, Karla did not meet eligibility for special education services as a child with a learning disability because she displayed the characteristics of a child with a more pervasive disorder, a general learning difficulty. In fact, it was noted in the evaluation report that Karla was not experiencing *unexpected* underachievement, which is a hallmark characteristic of children with learning disabilities. Instead, her underachievement was *expected* due to overall low cognitive abilities. Aside from the question regarding whether her overall cognitive abilities are actually low enough to be considered "pervasively low," one cannot argue against Karla's need for a significant amount of assistance in school. Though amazing, the fact that she does not qualify for special education services and supports as a child with a learning disability is much more complex than it may seem: She is also ineligible for *any* special education services and supports because there is no disability eligibility category into which she fits.

DISCUSSION AND RECOMMENDATIONS

Herein lies the issue: Why do students who have average to above average cognitive abilities qualify for special education services as students with learning disabilities (LDs), but students who are pervasively low functioning are not provided such supports? Both groups struggle academically, but students who are pervasively low functioning, those who are "swimming as fast as they can," do not qualify for specialized instruction. These are the students who may require accommodated or modified instruction and remediation of deficit skills (Shaw, 2010). They may also require smaller class sizes to allow for more one-on-one direct instruction. Instead, these students are left in the general education setting with no specialized instruction and no special education supports because they "do not qualify" for such services.

In the late 1960s, a conference was held regarding mental retardation and the education of students with this condition. Notes from the conference were published in a presidential report that identified a certain type of student as "The Six Hour Retarded Child" (President's Committee on Mental Retardation, 1969). There was an acknowledgement in the report that these students have significant difficulties in schools but may fare much better outside of the academic environment (i.e., the six-hour window of time when the child is in school). This report also acknowledged that these students do not receive necessary academic supports in schools and made seven recommendations to the public education system:

1. Expand programming for early childhood aged children
2. Increase parent and child involvement in the public school system
3. Restructure and retrain school staff
4. Reexamine then-present methods of conducting cognitive assessments and classification
5. Commit substantial financial resources to the education and support for said students
6. Hold schools accountable for educating all children, and
7. Involve parents, school staff, communities, and children in education. (p. 7).

Though not all of these recommendations address slow learners specifically, several of them do, and it is quite noteworthy that in almost 50 years we have been exceedingly unsuccessful at their implementation.

A decade-long study was completed by the conservative think tank Thomas D. Fordham Institute (Scull & Winkler, 2011) that addressed special education issues related to identification rates, funding, and personnel from the first decade of this millennium. Scull and Winkler reported that the overall population of students who received special education services decreased from 13.3% of the total United States student population in the 2000–2001 school year to 13.1% in 2009–2010, in large part due to a substantial drop in the percentage of children with specific learning disabilities: 6.1% of the total United States student population in the 2000–2001 school year vs. 4.9% in 2009–2010. These numbers vary considerably by state. For example, in Texas, where Karla was in school, those numbers look more drastic: The number of students receiving special education services in 2000–2001 was recorded as 12.1%, but this number dropped to 9.1% in 2009–2010. Only 3.8% of students in Texas were identified as having a specific learning disability in 2009–2010, compared to 4.9% nationwide (Scull & Winkler, 2011).

Scull and Winkler (2011) highlighted that Texas has declined in its special education student body (including the percentage of students with specific learning disabilities) over a 10-year period. They attributed this to several factors. First, Texas's practice of not identifying dyslexia as a specific learning disability eligible for special education funding may contribute to artificially low rates of specific learning disabilities. In Texas, students with dyslexia are provided instructional accommodations through Section 504 of the Rehabilitation Act of 1973. Second, Texas does not use the optional 13th disability category, "developmental delay," which includes a host of physical, cognitive, and other developmental issues that do not fall under other disability categories. The authors did not mention changes in identification methods, but one cannot rule out the use of the PSW approach as an additional reason for the decline.

It is important to note that such rates did not drop because identification has gotten better or more precise, as some researchers would assert. Moreover, stricter criteria do not necessarily mean more accurate criteria; in the case of LDs, it seems that, in this age of *in*clusion in our public school system, disability diagnosis has become much more *ex*clusive. In years prior, evaluators could simply choose a cognitive battery and achievement assessment battery that would likely elicit the necessary discrepancy for struggling students, including those who were slow learners. Now, evaluators must assess all areas of cognitive functioning differently in adherence with CHC theoretical practices, so Karla, who may have been eligible in years past and benefitted from specialized programming, no longer qualifies and now is simply labeled a slow learner and left to her own devices to struggle.

Interestingly enough, Karla may actually have been deemed intellectually disabled 40 years ago, which would have made her eligible for special education services. Prior to 1973 when the Education for All Handicapped Children Act (EAHCA) was authorized, children with a profile like Karla's could have been eligible for special education services as students with "borderline mental retardation" (Luick & Senf, 1979, p. 5). However, when EAHCA was reauthorized in 1990 as the

Individuals with Disabilities Education Act, special education services for students such as Karla were eliminated because eligibility criteria were revised so that the cut-off for mental retardation was lowered from an IQ of 85 to an IQ of 70. This eliminated services to approximately 14% of the population (then and now), as defined by the classic bell curve (Shaw, 2010), and these children are still left without educational assistance 40 years later.

Though redefining what learning disabilities really are will help to alleviate the crushing blows dealt to children who so badly need assistance in schools, this is not the only solution to such a seemingly complex but basically simple problem. As outlined by EAHCA, all students in schools must be provided with a free appropriate public education (FAPE), including students who currently fall into this gray area identified as slow learners. Such students must be provided with educational opportunities that are meaningful, just as high achieving and capable students are. Simply disqualifying slow learners from special education is not productive, nor does it ensure FAPE for those students. These students are referred for a psychoeducational evaluation to determine special education eligibility because they are not responding to research-based intervention programs, and later, when they do not qualify for special education services because they are slow learners, they are returned to the same intervention programs that did not work. These students continue to struggle to meet grade-level standards; ultimately, they are a poor fit for the education that is being provided. With the current model, schools are expecting the student to fit into existing instructional models rather than providing instruction that fits the student. These students have not failed in schools; the schools have failed them.

The common thread for special education eligibility as a student with a learning disability throughout history has been the need for *unexpected* underachievement, not simply underachievement. Essentially, if we expect a student to fail and he or she fails, then we are not liable, but if we do not expect a student to fail and he or she fails, then we have a problem. This logic is faulty. The law does not allow us to simply "pick and choose" the students we can help to avoid failure—we are supposed to be educating *all* of them.

The current way we are defining and subsequently providing special education services for students with LDs involves significant standardized assessment to target areas of deficit, which should then drive instruction. While this type of psychoeducational evaluation can be quite beneficial instructionally for the student being evaluated and the teachers who teach that student, students with LDs may not always be in need of highly specialized instruction that can only be delivered by someone trained in the area of special education. Moreover, students who meet current eligibility criteria as LD may actually respond very well to intervention approaches, as these students possess overall average to above average cognitive abilities that may compensate for the cognitive weaknesses. For example, a child who has average intellectual abilities in all areas with the exception of short term memory generally will perform well in school if the short-term memory deficit is handled. Targeted instruction and compensatory strategies that help to alleviate these short-term memory deficits are extraordinarily beneficial, and once the student is taught to access and use these techniques, the student will usually be academically successful.

However, a student who is a slow learner will struggle regardless of targeted intervention. School is difficult; academic tasks are supremely challenging. Intervention practices usually prove ineffective because these students do not possess the necessary cognitive abilities to handle academic tasks. As such, these are the students who do, in fact, require special education supports such as remedial instruction, slower pacing, smaller class sizes, and specifically targeted instruction. Why are we not simply providing appropriate instruction to all students instead of requiring special education eligibility as a prerequisite and thus excluding a substantial number of students from such appropriate instruction?

If we are going to require LD eligibility for special education services, we must revamp the way we are defining LD. Scanlon (2013) suggests that a new definition of LD must be developed to include all children who are struggling to learn in schools because "LD is a real disability, not just an academic problem" (p. 29). Furthermore, Scanlon notes that any definition of LD must acknowledge the difficulties within the home, school, and work settings, along with everyday living, as LD affects more than just reading, writing, and math. The current definition is insufficient and too exclusive in that students who truly are slow to learn and struggling in schools are not provided with any services or supports to make them academically successful. Rather, they are simply cast off as slow learners—as someone else's problem. Instead of using such a narrowed approach to eligibility, which Algozzine and

Ysseldyke (1987) call "entitlement decisions" (p. 310) rather than eligibility decisions, educators should be allowed to identify what students need to be successful and provide the necessary tools to make that success happen, without requiring that students be labeled as "learning disabled" to receive the instruction and assistance they need.

Alternatively, including an additional eligibility category for these students may be a viable solution. While identification as "intellectually disabled" may not be appropriate for students like Karla because students with slow learner profiles are generally more capable than this label suggests, encasing all struggling learners as "learning disabled" may also not be appropriate, particularly with the current trend of identifying students with LDs as those with *specific* LDs. Instead, it may be more appropriate to define such students as Flanagan et al. (2013) do: students with *general learning difficulty* or "GLD" (p. 268). This definition may provide practitioners with more valuable information about current levels of academic functioning and innate capabilities that could drive instructional and educational programming.

We currently do not have a special education category that includes slow learners, and it seems that this do-nothing approach is accepted because this is the way things have been done since the inception of the LD construct. In schools, particularly in the world of psychoeducational evaluations, we have always known that this problem existed; however, we tend to shrug our shoulders and cast a blind eye to the students who are affected by this. In speaking with colleagues, we often cite how "sad" it is for students like Karla, but we do nothing to move beyond the trite admission.

Kavale, Holdnack, and Mostert (2005) would argue that "[slow learners] have never been a special education category and probably never should" (p. 5). These researchers support the exclusive nature of the LD construct. While they often reference students who would be identified as slow learners, they do not acknowledge the slow learning child as one who requires special supports and services, nor do they offer any solutions to the issue. In fact, Kavale and colleagues would suggest that special education is remedial by design and slow learners cannot be remediated; slow learners are experiencing difficulties that cannot be helped, so providing them with remedial education is futile. This notion perpetuates social injustice, as it negates the requirement that we provide an appropriate education to all students in our public education system. How "appropriate" is it to allow a student to move through grade-level curriculum without ever having been taught to read on a functional level so that he or she could pass a driver's license exam, for example?

Students who are low functioning but are categorically "too low" for LD and "too high" to be considered intellectually disabled cannot continue to be ignored. We cannot continue to wait around for "someone else" to educate these students in a meaningful and appropriate manner that provides them with the necessary life skills (such as the ability to read) to be productive members of society. Much was written about this issue immediately after the 1973 legislation and again after the authorization of IDEA in 1990; however, since then, little research on the topic exists. Instead, a significant amount of research has been done to assist in assessment and evaluation of learning disabilities as they are now defined. In fact, new assessment materials were published in 2014 that specifically and thoroughly address the PSW approach to LD eligibility. While these steps may be significantly beneficial to students who have overall average to above average ability and who display cognitive deficits in one or two assessed areas of intelligence, this approach does nothing to help the slow learners who do not meet eligibility for special education services.

Ignoring these students is irresponsible at best because we have a social obligation to ensure that all students are provided with an education that leads to productive and manageable adult lives. Slow learning students struggle well beyond early elementary school; indeed, they often drop out of high school (Shaw, 2010). Those who do graduate from high school may do so without functional academic skills such as reading and calculating change. According to Shaw (2010), this group of students "makes up approximately 14% of the school population . . . more than students in all special education categories combined" (p. 12). We cannot continue to deny appropriate and meaningful educational experiences to such a large portion of our students in our public school systems.

REFERENCES

Algozzine, B., & Ysseldkye, J. (1987). Questioning discrepancies: Retaking the first step 20 years later. *Learning Disability Quarterly, 10*(4), 201–312.

Coomer, L. F. (2015). Definitions and criteria used by state education departments for identifying specific learning disabilities (Unpublished specialist project). Western Kentucky University, Bowling Green, KY.

Education for All Handicapped Children Act of 1975, Pub. L. No. 94-142, 89 Stat. 773 (1975).

Flanagan, D., Ortiz, S., & Alfonso, V. (2006). *Essentials of cross-battery assessment (2nd Ed.)*. NJ: John Wiley & Sons.

Flanagan, D., Ortiz, S., & Alfonso, V. (2013). *Essentials of cross-battery assessment (3rd ed.)*. NJ: John Wiley & Sons.

Individuals with Disabilities Education Improvement Act of 2004, Part B, 34 C.F.R. § 300 (Electronic Code of Federal Regulations, 2016).

Kaufman, A. S., & Kaufman, N. L. (2004). *Kaufman Assessment Battery for Children* (2nd ed.). Circle Pines, MN: American Guidance Service.

Kavale, K., Holdnack, J., & Mostert, M. (2005). Responsiveness to intervention and the identification of specific learning disability: A critique and alternative proposal. *Learning Disability Quarterly, 28*, 2–16.

Kaznowski, K. (2004). *Slow learners: Are educators leaving them behind? NASSP Bulletin, 88*(641), 31–45.

Luick, A. H., & Senf, G. M. (1979). Where have all the children gone? *Journal of Learning Disabilities, 12*(5), 285–287.

Pearson Education, Inc. (2009). *K-8 technical manual, Developmental Reading Assessment* (2nd ed.). Upper Saddle River, NJ: Author.

Peltopuro, M., Ahonen, T., Kaartinen, J., Seppala, H., & Narhi, V. (2014). Borderline intellectual functioning: A systematic literature review. *Intellectual and Developmental Disabilities. 52*(6), 419-443.

President's Committee on Mental Retardation. (1969). *The six-hour retarded Child. A report on a conference on problems of education of children in the inner city.* Washington, DC: Bureau of Education for the Handicapped. Retrieved from http://files.eric.ed.gov/fulltext/ED038827.pdf

Scanlon, D. (2013). Specific learning disability and its newest definition: Which is comprehensive? And which is insufficient? *Journal of Learning Disabilities, 46*(1), 26–33.

Schrank, F. A., McGrew, K. S., & Mather, N. (2014a). *Woodcock-Johnson IV tests of achievement.* Rolling Meadows, IL: Riverside.

Schrank, F. A., McGrew, K. S., & Mather, N. (2014b). *Woodcock-Johnson IV tests of cognitive abilities.* Rolling Meadows, IL: Riverside.

Scull, J., & Winkler, A. M. (2011). *Shifting trends in special education.* Thomas Fordham Institute.

Shaw, S. R. (2010). Rescuing students from the slow learner trap. *Principal Leadership.* February. 12–16.

Wieland, J., & Zitman, F. (2016). It is time to bring borderline intellectual functioning back into the main fold of classification systems. *BJ Psych Bulletin, 40*(204-206).

Chapter 3

THE SOCIAL CONUNDRUM: EMOTIONAL DISTURBANCE VS. SOCIAL MALADJUSTMENT

Griselda Landeros Wells

INTRODUCTION

In order for behaviorally challenged students to receive specialized services and supports in the school setting through special education programming, they must be identified under guidelines from the Individuals with Disabilities Education Improvement Act (IDEIA) of 2004 as being Emotionally Disturbed (ED). Students with behavioral problems who do not meet the eligibility criteria for this educational label are many times categorized as Socially Maladjusted (SM). These students often do not receive the help they need despite their many behavioral problems, leaving teachers and school administrators struggling to deal with the challenges brought about by the misbehavior of these students (Hochbaum, 2011). While ED students will go on to have specialized programming such as behavior intervention plans, behavioral accommodations, and even specialized classrooms for those with the most challenging behaviors, the SM students fall between the cracks of the education system—a system that is supposed to provide a free appropriate public education (FAPE) to all students.

In order to understand this exclusion from services, one must look to federal guidelines that stipulate the eligibility criteria for ED. In order to be considered a student with an ED, the student

> [must exhibit] one or more of the following characteristics over a long period of time and to a marked degree that adversely affects a child's

57

educational performance: (A) An inability to learn that cannot be explained by intellectual, sensory, or health factors, (B) An inability to build or maintain satisfactory interpersonal relationships with peers and teachers, (C) Inappropriate types of behaviors or feelings under normal circumstances, (D) A general pervasive mood of unhappiness or depression, and (E) A tendency to develop physical symptoms or fears associated with personal or school problems. Emotional Disturbance includes schizophrenia. The term does not apply to children who are socially maladjusted, unless it is determined that they have an emotional disturbance. (34 C.F.R., §300.8, (c)(4))

Therefore, if a student meets eligibility for ED, the gateway to special education supports and services is open; for those considered SM and falling under the exclusionary clause, such as students clinically diagnosed with Oppositional Defiant Disorder or Conduct Disorder, the gates are closed and entry into the realm of special education is denied. The number of students who are left without these much needed supports and services is unknown, as there is no required tracking system in place at the state or federal levels (Cloth, Evans, Becker, & Paternite, 2013).

What is known is the number of students who have behavioral problems in the school setting and end up in the juvenile justice system. The majority of youth involved in the juvenile justice system were repeat offenders in the school setting. Texas Appleseed (Fowler, Lightsey, Monger, & Aseltine, 2010) surveyed 400 students incarcerated in Texas Youth Commission (TYC) facilities, at-risk students, and a group of students in a program for children with leadership qualities; the latter two groups had never been involved in the TYC system. The authors found that 56% of those who had been incarcerated indicated having been involved in 10 or more in-school suspensions (ISS), versus 24% of at-risk youth not involved in TYC. Out-of-School suspensions (OSS) were reported by 46% of the TYC respondents versus 15% of those who had not been a part of TYC. A staggering 73% of students confined in the juvenile justice system reported previously being sent to their school district's alternative education center/program, compared to 42% of non-TYC youth (Fowler, Lightsey, Monger, & Aseltine, 2010). Although this study used a relatively small sample, the results do point to a sharp contrast between incarcerated and nonincarcerated youth as well as the high rates of enforcement of "zero-tolerance" policies in public schools.

The evidence linking discipline problems in the school setting and involvement in the juvenile justice system is overwhelmingly apparent. Also apparent is the lack of programming, services, and supports provided for students who are repeat offenders. This group of behaviorally challenged students lacks appropriate services to meet their needs.

Many times the SM students are expelled or suspended from school as an intervention to their behavior problems. While removing a student from school is by no means an intervention, this discipline method appears to help teachers and administrators rid themselves of the problem, albeit temporarily. ED students, on the other hand, while still receiving consequences such as suspension, have these punishments doled out to a lesser degree. The reason for this disparity is that schools must follow protocols that mandate practices such as administration of functional behavior assessments (FBAs) in order to develop or modify behavior intervention plans (BIPs) prior to continued changes of placement (e.g., suspension) for ED students. These changes of placement from the students' current placement to more restrictive settings (such as from school to home due to suspensions) must be addressed at Manifestation Determination multidisciplinary team meetings, which determine whether the conduct violation stems from the school's failure to implement the IEP and whether the conduct is connected to the student's disability (34 C.F.R. § 300.530(e)). Such requirements are not in place for SM students–they can simply be suspended and expelled with no protocols needed other than a phone call home to have parents pick up their behaviorally challenged child from school. But how did such a disparity arise?

BACKGROUND

The Social Maladjustment Exclusionary Clause

According to data presented by the U.S. Department of Education in its 37th Annual Report to Congress on the implementation of the Individuals with Disabilities Education Act (2015), 5,734,393 students, ages six through 21, were identified as being served under their school district's special education program. Of these students, 6.0% or 344,064 were identified as having an ED. While not the largest group of students with disabilities, the ED population had the highest percentage

of students receiving school removals, in-school and out-of-school suspensions, and expulsions. Leading states in removals to interim alternative educational settings are Texas, Kansas, Pennsylvania, and
Washington, with West Virginia, Arkansas, and Michigan reporting the
least number of removals (United States Department of Education,
2015). In short, although the ED population makes up a small percentage of the identified special education population, they are the ones receiving the highest frequency of disciplinary consequences resulting in
nonprovision of services in the general education setting. Not included
in these statistics, however, are the countless SM students who do not
receive the specialized school supports that they require due to an exclusionary clause.

Why did this exclusionary clause that neglects to take into consideration so many students in need come about to begin with? Bower's
(1957) study of more than 6,000 children (elementary through high
school) defined characteristics of students with ED. Of those children,
207 of them were previously diagnosed with a mental health condition
and were receiving mental health services. This was a fact not known
by their teachers, who as part of the study submitted data that determined the key behavioral differences between the students already diagnosed and receiving mental health services and those who were not
displaying atypical behavior difficulties. The results brought about the
five characteristics currently included in the Federal definition of ED
(Barnett, 2012). However, the SM clause was added to the Federal definition, it is believed, in order to "satisfy the concerns of legislators and
educational administrators who did not want schools to be mandated
to provide services to delinquent and antisocial youth, a notoriously
difficult to reach population" (Merrell & Walker, 2004, p. 901). Bower
himself disagreed with the insertion of the exclusionary clause, as have
other researchers in the field who argue that it is not possible for a student to be socially maladjusted without also exhibiting characteristics
of an ED (Merrell & Walker, 2004).

To this day, after over 40 years (as the guidelines for ED eligibility
were first introduced in 1975 with the inception of the Education for
All Handicapped Children Act), there does not exist a single, widely-
accepted definition of SM. Nonetheless, those who have attempted to
differentiate SM from ED have concluded that SM encompasses behaviors that constitute "a pattern of engagement in purposive antisocial, destructive, and delinquent behavior" (Merrell & Walker, 2004, p.

901); the key word here is "purposive." There is a notion that SM students "engage in antisocial behavior in a willful manner . . . as a way to maintain or enhance their social status within the antisocial subgroup, and in a manner that is unlawful" (Merrell & Walker, 2014, p. 902). Proponents of excluding SM from the ED definition suggest that this purposive and willful aspect of the behavior of SM students is what differentiates them from the ED group, in that the behaviors of the latter group are not necessarily of their choosing.

Lack of Understanding

Contributing to this perception that SM behaviors are within the control of the student whereas ED behaviors are not is the internalizing/externalizing behavior dichotomy (Achenbach, 1978). The behavioral characteristics of those who are identified as ED students are for the most part equated with internalizing behaviors, related to clear emotional dysregulation difficulties, such as depression and anxiety. In contrast, students with SM characteristics display externalizing behaviors such as those associated with inattention, hyperactivity, impulsivity, and oppositionality. Both internalizing and externalizing behaviors have a biological component and are heavily influenced by environmental factors (e.g., Deater-Deckard & Dodge, 1997; Ge et al., 1996; Mash & Barkley, 2014). Both categories of behavior are associated with emotion dysregulation and are influenced by a complex system of internal and external factors. Furthermore, there is considerable overlap between both categories of behaviors, with some estimates suggesting substantial comorbidity (e.g., Cosgrove et al., 2011; Levy, Hawes, & Johns, 2015). The perception that SM behaviors are "chosen," whereas ED behaviors are not, is a vast oversimplification of a complex issue. Yet it remains an influential view.

This view underlies the belief that SM children are delinquent youth whom the school system has no responsibility for and whose needs are beyond help. A related belief is that SM youth are simply too volatile and that their behaviors cannot be corrected as they are socially rather than emotionally based (Sullivan & Sadeh, 2014). In contrast, there are those who argue that the term "emotional" in the ED eligibility criteria should be used inclusively to convey any underlying factors associated with behavioral problems, which would increase eligibility and access to services among SM students (Forness & Knitzer, 1992). The ED vs.

SM debate has been ongoing, and despite the lack of guidance on what social maladjustment is (or is not), states continue to use the SM exclusionary clause when making their eligibility determinations for ED. Of the 50 States and the District of Columbia, only four states include SM in their ED eligibility criteria; the others all use the SM exclusionary clause in determining their ED special education student population (Sullivan & Sadeh, 2014). In light of these exclusions, the needs of difficult-to-reach SM youth continue to be overlooked–due to lack of understanding, a lack of adequate programming, and a lack of incentive to change the status quo.

A general lack of understanding of what ED and SM are and how to manage these complex behaviors has resulted in many students not receiving a free appropriate public education. Foremost among factors contributing to lack of understanding would be inadequate teacher training, as classroom teachers are the first line of defense and chief behavioral intervention implementers. Are teachers adequately trained to deal with seriously behaviorally challenged students in the general education classroom setting, or even in the special education classroom? Abebe and Hailemariam (2007) found that inadequate training as well as lack of support was reported by classroom teachers. The lack of effective classroom management often leads to further behavior problems, thus compounding a never-ending cycle of ineffective practices used to deal with the most challenging of students. Cassady (2011) reported that teachers were more willing to work with students with disabilities such as autism versus students with emotional/behavioral disorders. Major classroom concerns for teachers include provision of effective classroom discipline and how to successfully handle the behavior of disruptive students (Richardson & Shupe, 2003). Other studies have found teachers to have high levels of stress, with teachers reporting "feelings of frustration, anger, exhaustion, being upset, and/or being at a loss" (Male, 2003, p. 169). Perhaps more training at the college/university level is needed in order to better prepare future teachers for teaching students with significant behavior difficulties, as teachers clearly do not feel prepared to adequately handle such students.

Lack of Programming

However, educators and teacher training programs do not bear sole responsibility for the problem. Even among well-informed educators, there is a very real concern that must be considered when educating these two similar yet very different student populations, as the two groups have vastly different needs. If both of these distinct groups were to be combined into one, what would adequate programming look like? At present, specialized classrooms are available to provide services for students with ED; the more severe the behaviors, the more services are provided and possibly the more time spent in these classrooms with lower student-to-teacher ratios. If a student with SM who is oppositional and antisocial is placed into this classroom, what would happen to the emotionally volatile ED student who may be suffering from depression, anxiety, and low-self-esteem? There is genuine concern that two very different types of students with diverse needs that require distinct programming would end up in one place, being taught in the same manner and using the same type of intervention strategies. It would definitely simplify programming and ensure more positive outcomes if educators continue to focus solely on the ED category without adding SM students into the mix. Some would also argue that it is unfair to the most volatile of ED students who are dealing with emotional instability to have one more issue (i.e., SM classmates) to deal with. On the other hand, is it fair to deny services to students simply because the logistics are complicated? Many of the needs of SM students can be addressed through evidence-based interventions such as increased academic supports to increase school success and curtail behavior difficulties, self-management interventions such as goal-setting, anger management strategies, and problem-solving strategies (Hanover Research, 2013). Early intervention and appropriate programming that addresses the unique needs of SM students can benefit this group while not hampering the progress of ED students.

Lack of Incentive

Perhaps the most troubling of all factors that contribute to the exclusion of SM students from services is the lack of incentive to change the status quo. Currently, the long-term outcomes for students with behavioral challenges—whether related to SM or ED—are discouraging. Not only are they suspended or expelled at higher rates than their peers without disabilities, they end up in the juvenile justice system at higher percentages than their peers. Of students in the juvenile justice system who were identified as having special education eligibilities, up to 48% were identified as having an ED (Mallett, 2016). The National Center on Criminal Justice and Disability (2015) reports that 65%-70% of youth involved in the justice system have a disability. Similarly, findings by the National Collaborative on Workforce and Disability (2015) reports 66% of male detainees and 74% of female detainees in the juvenile justice system meet the diagnostic criteria for one or more psychiatric disorders. These numbers do not include youth with Conduct Disorders (those typically falling under the SM category) because of the frequency with which they are involved in the juvenile justice system. Thus, it appears that even those who should be identified as ED are often ending up in the juvenile justice system. These findings are inexcusable, given that these youth are supposed to be served in the school setting and provided with a free appropriate public education with the provision of specialized supports, interventions, and accommodations. Students with disabilities, in particular emotional and behavioral problems, are being funneled into the justice system at an alarming rate.

As these statistics show, our educational system already has difficulties with ensuring successful outcomes for ED students, as this special education subpopulation has the poorest outcomes in many areas as compared to other disability categories (Merrell & Walker, 2004). There are those who argue that removing the SM exclusion clause would open the doors and allow a free-for-all pass to special education for the most difficult students to rehabilitate (Becker, Weist, & Evans, 2011). The fear is that this would cause a cascade of issues to contend with such as teacher training, additional staff requirements, and expensive to implement programming such as separate classrooms and mental health services by adequately trained/licensed professionals. While school systems have legitimate budget issues to contend with, it is ironic that the organizations that are in place to help these students succeed are the same ones that have an array of rationalizations to inhibit their success in the name of fiscal responsibility. The view of SM students as budding criminals who cannot be helped protects the status quo by focusing only on those students for whom we can ensure an adequate level of success at the lowest cost.

CASE STUDY

DJ was a 14-year-old, middle school student who was becoming increasingly more difficult to control in the school setting. He had been involved with the authorities due to possession of controlled substances in school as well as for truancy and disrespect towards teachers and school administrators. DJ had three teachers from whom he would take directives and redirection. With much persuasion, he would complete a very limited number of assignments for these three teachers. He treated the rest of his teachers with disrespect, as evidenced by rude comments, talking back, and the use of curse words in class, towards both the teachers and his peers. DJ would often walk out of class or simply leave campus between classes. He was also failing all subjects due to absences and lack of work completion.

DJ was referred for a psychological evaluation to determine eligibility for special education as an Emotionally Disturbed student. His evaluation revealed lack of support in the home: no father involvement, mother present sporadically throughout the month, being raised by his elderly grandparents who have no control over his behaviors, and an older relative in the home who was recently released from prison for drug and theft offenses. All behavioral scales administered indicated behaviors consistent with a conduct disorder. He was found to be knowledgeable of social conventions yet chose to disregard societal rules and norms. In school he would comply with teachers and adults he perceived as caring and attentive to his needs. He was contemptuous of and disrespectful towards those teachers and adults who were confrontational towards him and did not display an interest in his personal needs. DJ was part of a social group made up of other students and young adults who were also involved in delinquency; he understood the consequences of his actions yet chose to continue his involvement in such behaviors. DJ did not display symptomatology consistent with depression or anxiety, and he was not withdrawn or alienated from others. Table 3.1 presents the eligibility criteria for emotional disturbance and DJ's results.

DJ spent most of the week at a friend's house where there was limited to no adult supervision. He was out of the house evenings and nights and had begun to spend a great deal of time with older, known gang members. Despite his behavioral problems in school and the community, he did not meet eligibility as a student with an Emotional

Table 3.1
ED ELIGIBILITY CRITERIA AND RESULTS

Criterion	*Results*
(A) An inability to learn that cannot be explained by intellectual, sensory, or health factors	*Criterion not met:* Although the student was displaying failing grades and overall poor academic performance, his intellectual ability and academic functioning on standardized tests was assessed to be within the average range. He was choosing not to complete assignments and to skip school, which caused him to be assigned failing grades in all classes.
(B) An inability to build or maintain satisfactory interpersonal relationships with peers and teachers	*Criterion not met:* The student was able to build and maintain friendships; he was a part of a large social group of peers and was able to build rapport and positive relationships with a few teachers he had bonded with.
(C) Inappropriate types of behaviors or feelings under normal circumstances	*Criterion not met:* Although DJ did display inappropriate behavior or feelings under normal circumstances, these behaviors were consistent with patterns of behavior consistent with his social peer group; his home situation was marred by instability and his inappropriate behaviors or feelings under normal circumstances were controlled by the situations he was in (e.g., certain teachers received respect and good behavior, while others did not).
(D) A general pervasive mood of unhappiness or depression	*Criterion not met:* DJ did not exhibit symptomatology consistent with sadness or depression. He was not withdrawn or alienated from others, and he did not exhibit characteristics of anxiety. Behavioral scales did not indicate elevated scores in regards to these areas.
(E) A tendency to develop physical symptoms or fears associated with personal or school problems.	*Criterion not met:* There was no symptomatology consistent with any type of physical disorder linked to a psychological factor or conflict. There were no medical issues without evident medical findings.

Disturbance; rather he was considered a Socially Maladjusted student who displayed primarily externalizing behaviors. Another student entering the school-to-prison pipeline, perhaps? This child *has* been left behind.

DISCUSSION AND RECOMMENDATIONS

Early Detection and Intervention

Several concerns arise in relation to this case. First, there is a "wait to fail" issue; DJ was 14 years old and in middle school. School records indicate his problem behaviors had been ongoing since his late elementary school years. DJ began to be suspended from school in the 3rd grade when he started acting out and becoming aggressive towards his teachers when angered. On many occasions he would be sent to sit in the front office and "wait" for the principal to discipline him. While in the office, he would be treated kindly by front office staff while he waited. The class-office-wait for principal cycle became routine, and soon his mother or grandparents were being called to pick him up from school. His grandmother quickly became his primary caretaker while his mother was at work. He would often be paid to behave and then taken to a convenience store to purchase a treat for behaving.

Time spent out of class and suspensions from school began to take their toll on his academic progress, and soon, not only was he receiving failing grades, he was still misbehaving. It was not until sixth grade that he was placed in Response to Intervention (RTI), and a behavior plan was developed. His behavior plan included lofty goals of reducing inappropriate language and completing all class assignments. However, instead of positive behavior supports, punishments were put into place as consequences: being sent to in-school suspensions, conferences with his mother, and being sent to the principal's office (despite the ineffectiveness of this consequence in the past). During this time, negative behaviors out of school began to increase, as did delinquent behaviors in the community. DJ was picked up by the police for breaking a window of an empty building with a group of his friends and for trespassing in a skate park after hours. Both times he was released to his mother and no further criminal consequences were recorded. In eight grade, DJ "bragged" to teachers that he was involved in gang activity, including criminal drug-related activity. Attempts by the school counselors and administrators to have the student's parent become more involved in his life were unsuccessful. His mother and grandparents have shown up to school only on occasion, and they have become increasingly difficult to contact via phone.

In general, DJ has fallen victim to suspensions and expulsions. Now that his behaviors have begun to escalate to the breaking point, there is an urgency to label him in order to provide him with specialized supports and services. As with many others in his situation, there is a reactive response to addressing his behaviors. The practice of repeated suspensions, which amounts to punishment rather than true intervention, was found to be ineffective (which should surprise no one). Policies that "automatically suspend or expel students for certain behaviors or infractions can be particularly harmful to students with conduct disorders, as expulsion and suspension effectively remove already troubled or disengaged students from the academic setting" (Hanover Research, 2013, p. 5). In the case of DJ, removing him from the school setting also meant removing him from adult supervision, meals, and any type of supportive adult he could reach out to.

Need for Support

Now that DJ has been found to be a "DNQ" (does not qualify for special education services) will there be any significant changes made to his programming, or will he continue to get a free day (or two, or three) out of school? More of the same is obviously not the answer. However, without a system in place to address the needs of students like DJ, who fall between the cracks of our education system, continued failure will be the norm. A strong RTI program that provides a tiered system of positive behavior supports, with concentrated interventions for the most behaviorally challenged students, would be ideal. However, such a system can only work if it is carried out with integrity and fidelity. There must also be sound progress monitoring in place as this will determine levels of support needed: "A student should be considered eligible for more intensive support services based on an inadequate response to a multitiered system of interventions" (Gresham, 2007, p. 221). As new, more targeted interventions are attempted, data should be collected to determine effectiveness and programming changes should be made accordingly in order to ensure success.

DJ had very limited parental involvement in (or out of) the school setting. Parental support issues must be addressed to further ensure the attainment of successful outcomes. Granted, this is by far the most difficult factor to control as one cannot regulate the home environment; nevertheless, attempts should be made to strengthen the school-home bond. Research has shown "that schools that engage in parent involvement programs tend to see immediate and positive results from their efforts. In fact, almost no examples exist of school-sponsored parent involvement programs of any nature NOT succeeding in their intended goals" (Dwyer & Hecht, 1992, p. 275). Regardless of how difficult it may be to involve some parents in the education of their children, some parental involvement is better than no parental involvement.

Effective Programming

It is essential to address the need for changes in programming to meet the needs of students with emotional and behavioral problems. A variety of programming options should be implemented based on a tiered system that incorporates evidence-based strategies and specialized training for teachers should be provided to all educators working with the ED and SM populations (Lewis, 2016). These strategies and supports represent more tailored interventions such as those found within a second tier (small group supports) or third tier (individualized supports) of an RTI system. Access to mentorship programs such as *Check-In, Check-Out* (Todd, Campbell, Meyer, & Homer, 2008) give behaviorally challenged students an opportunity to build a supportive relationship with an adult in the school setting would significantly increase a student's support network. The designated adult would be available on a daily basis to help not only with academic needs but with emotional, social, family, and community needs as well. A system for out-of-school support might include services provided by a school-based social worker who could help guide not only the student but the family in regards to resources available in the community (mental health services, individual and family counseling, guidance in regards to legal support, and assistance with daily living issues – food banks, clothing, etc.). An increase in "professional responsibility to all students" (Sullivan & Sadeh, 2014, p. 454) and parental accountability in the successful outcomes of behaviorally challenged students is the first step in supporting the most volatile of student populations. Although these intervention recommendations would take additional staff support, the possibility of improved outcomes far exceeds the current outcomes for the behaviorally challenged, in particular the SM student population.

Epilogue

After receiving DNQ status, DJ's school worked with its school psychologist to develop a behavior intervention plan containing reasonable goals with positive behavior supports incorporated into the plan. It was recommended that adults approach him in a nonconfrontational (nonargumentative) manner, provide him choices in assignments, adopt an "asking vs. telling" attitude when requesting that he complete an assignment, and stop speaking in a certain manner. It was also recommended that he be assigned a mentor (one of the teachers he has a positive relationship with) and that the school district's Parental Involvement Department become involved in trying to build a positive, working relationship with the family. A final recommendation included placing DJ in classes with smaller student-to-teacher ratios in order to help his teachers provide him with more individualized attention and instruction in an attempt to close the academic gaps that had begun in his elementary years.

After the behavior plan for DJ was implemented, there have been small successes in his behavior and school attendance. He now has a mentor teacher whom he can access during the school day and this same teacher has provided him with academic assistance. This in turn has caused some academic success, which has somewhat improved DJ's school attendance. His teachers were also hand-picked to ensure he would be enrolled in classes with teachers viewed as more compatible with him; this has decreased his instances of walking out of class. Parental involvement has continued to be almost non-existent despite attempts by school staff to involve the parent in parent/teacher meetings.

Although DJ's school put these appropriate interventions into place in spite of the lack of ED diagnosis, schools are not required to provide such services to SM students. The use of suspension, expulsion, and alternative educational programs appears to be the preferred method of managing students' problematic behaviors in many school districts (Fowler et al., 2010). In contrast, varied options to help diversify the road to graduation as well as RTI programming to address the behavioral needs of SM students (before these needs are beyond reasonable control) are underutilized. Above all else, there is the need for the reconsideration of eligibility criteria for special education services under the ED eligibility category. Current standards are closing the door on a multitude of students who are on an accelerated route to failure. If reconsideration of eligibility under Emotional Disturbance is not the answer, then consideration for an additional eligibility category should be investigated (Cloth et al., 2013). For now, the social conundrum of how best to serve SM students continues.

REFERENCES

Abebe, S., & Hailemariam, A. (2007). The challenges of managing student behavior problems in the classroom. Unpublished manuscript. Retrieved from https://eric.ed.gov/?id=ED494910

Achenbach, T. M. (1978). The Child Behavior Profile: I. Boys aged 6–11. *Journal of Consulting and Clinical Psychology, 46*(3), 478.

Barnett, D. (2012). A grounded theory for identifying students with emotional disturbance: Promising practices for assessment, intervention, and service delivery. *Contemporary School Psychology, 16*(1), p. 21–31.

Becker, S., P., Weist, M. D., & Evans, S. W. (2011). Eligibility, assessment, and educational placement issues for students classified with emotional disturbance: Federal and state-level analyses. *School Mental Health, 3*(24), 24–34.

Bower, E. M. (1957). A process for identifying disturbed children. *Children, 4*, 143–147.

Cassady, J. M. (2011). Teachers' attitudes toward the inclusion of students with autism and emotional behavioral disorder. *Electronic Journal for Inclusive Education, 2*(7), 1–23. Retrieved from http://corescholar.libraries.wright.edu/ejie

Cloth, A. H., Evans, S. W., Becker, S. P., & Paternite, C. E. (2013). Social maladjustment and special education: State regulations and continued controversy. *Journal of Emotional and Behavioral Disorders, 22*(4), 214–224.

Cosgrove, V. E., Rhee, S. H., Gelhorn, H. L., Boeldt, D., Corley, R. C., Ehringer, M. A., . . . Hewitt, J. K. (2011). Structure and etiology of co-occurring internalizing and externalizing disorders in adolescents. *Journal of Abnormal Child Psychology, 39*(1), 109–123.

Deater-Deckard, K., & Dodge, K. (1997). Externalizing behavior problems and discipline revisited: Nonlinear effects and variation by culture, context, and gender. *Psychological Inquiry, 8*(3), 161–175.

Dwyer, D. J., & Hecht, J. B. (1992). Minimal parental involvement: Causes underlying minimal parental involvement in the education of their children. *School Community Journal, 2* (2), p. 275–289.

Forness, S. R, & Knitzer, J. (1992). A new proposed definition and terminology to replace "serious emotional disturbance" in Individuals with Disabilities Education Act. *School Psychology Review, 21* (1), p. 12–20.

Fowler, D., Lightsey, R., Monger, J., & Aseltine, E. (2010). Texas' school to prison pipeline: Ticketing, arrest, and use of force in schools. Texas Appleseed, Austin, TX. Retrieved from www.texasappleseed.org

Ge, X., Conger, R. D., Cadoret, R. J., Neiderhiser, J. M., Yates, W., Troughton, E., & Stewart, M. A. (1996). The developmental interface between nature and nurture: A mutual influence model of child antisocial behavior and parent behaviors. *Developmental Psychology, 32*(4), 574–589.

Gresham, F. M. (2007). Response to intervention and emotional and behavioral disorders: Best practices in assessment for intervention. *Assessment for Effective Intervention, 32*(4), p. 214–222.

Hanover Research. (2013). *Effective programming for emotional and behavioral disorders.* Washington, DC: Author. Retrieved from https://www.district287.org/uploaded/A_Better_Way/EffectiveProgramsforEmotionalandBehavioralDisordersHanover2013.pdf

Hochbaum, D. (2011). Emotional disturbance and social maladjustment: Doing away with the IDEA's "Social Maladjustment Exclusionary Clause." Unpublished manuscript. Retrieved from http://www.luc.edu/media/lucedu/law/centers/childlaw/childed/pdfs/2011studentpapers/hochbaum_emotional.pdf

Individuals with Disabilities Education Improvement Act of 2004, 34 C.F.R. § 300.8 (c)(4) et seq. (Electronic Code of Federal Regulations, 2016).

Levy, F., Hawes, D. J., & Johns, A. (2015). Externalizing and internalizing comorbidity. In T. P. Beauchaine & S. P. Hinshaw (Eds.), *The Oxford handbook of externalizing spectrum disorders* (pp. 443–460). New York: Oxford University Press.

Lewis, T. J. (2016). Does the field of EBD need a distinct set of "intensive" interventions or more systemic intensity within a continuum of social/emotional supports? *Journal of Emotional and Behavioral Disorders, 24*(3), 187–190.

Male, D. (2003). Challenging behavior: The perceptions of teachers of children and young people with severe learning disabilities. *Journal of Research in Special Educational Needs, 3* (3), p. 162–171.

Mallett, C. A. (2016). The school to prison pipeline: Disproportionate impact on vulnerable children and adolescents. *Education and Urban Society, 33* (15).

Mash, E. J., & Barkley, R. A. (1994). *Child psychopathology* (3rd ed.). New York: The Guilford Press.

Merrell, K. W., & Walker, H. M. (2004). Deconstructing a definition: Social maladjustment versus emotional disturbance and moving the EBD field forward. *Psychology in Schools, 41* (8), p. 899–910.

National Center on Criminal Justice and Disability. (2015). *Justice-involved youth with intellectual and developmental disabilities: A call to action for the juvenile justice community.* Washington, DC: The Arc. Retrieved from http://www.thearc.org/file/15-037-Juvenile-Justice-White-Paper_2016.pdf

National Collaborative on Workforce and Disability. (2015). Youth involved in the juvenile corrections system. Retrieved from http://www.ncwd-youth.info/youth-in-juvenile-corrections

Richardson, B. C., & Shupe, M. J. (2003). The importance of teacher self-awareness in working with students with emotional and behavioral disorders. *Teaching Exceptional Children, 36*(2), 8–13.

Sullivan, A. L., & Sadeh, S. S. (2014). Differentiating social maladjustment from emotional disturbance: An analysis of case law. *School Psychology Review, 43*(4), 450–471.

Todd, A. W., Campbell, A. L., Meyer, G. G., & Horner, R. H. (2008). The effects of a targeted intervention to reduce problem behaviors elementary school implementation of check in-check out. *Journal of Positive Behavior Interventions, 10*(1), 46–55.

U.S. Department of Education, Office of Special Education and Rehabilitative Services, Office of Special Education Programs. (2015). *37th Annual Report to Congress on the Implementation of the Individuals with Disabilities Education Act, 2015.* Washington, D.C. 2015. Retrieved from http://www.ed.gov/about/reports/annual/osep

Chapter 4

DISABILITY, DISADVANTAGE, OR DISCRIMINATION?

Kanisha Porter and Nicole McZeal Walters

INTRODUCTION

Students from environmentally disadvantaged homes face numerous problems on a regular basis in their academic settings. Poverty-related factors such as poor nutrition, inadequate healthcare, unsafe living conditions, and parents who are undereducated and overwhelmed are related to disadvantaged students' low academic performance, behavioral and social challenges, and high absenteeism (Jensen, 2009). Consequently, these problems frequently lead to a referral for special education that ultimately ends with eligibility criteria being met. Environmentally disadvantaged students are more likely to be labeled and placed in special education classes because of evaluators' failure to consider environmental and/or sociological factors that may be contributing to low academic performance (Coutinho & Oswald, 2004).

Mislabeling within special education is a violation of children's dignity and rights. Children should not be identified for special education on the basis of economic challenges beyond their control, scarce resources, or any other environmental influence that may be negatively impacting their academic performance. Such inappropriate labeling of disadvantaged students is a recurring problem that continues to contribute to the disproportionate representation of students of color in special education (U.S. Department of Education, 2016), as rates of low socioeconomic status are higher among Hispanic and African American children than among Caucasian children (Patten & Krogstad, 2015).

Furthermore, although environmental factors related to socioeconomic status may be related to disproportionate representation of students of color, the role of implicit cultural bias and other classroom-related variables cannot be overlooked (Blair, 2002). If students are to receive an appropriate education, educators must do a better job of differentiating between a true disability condition and socioeconomic disadvantage while also acknowledging the potential for bias and discrimination in the referral, assessment, and placement processes.

BACKGROUND

Special Education Eligibility and Sociological Rule-Outs

The Individuals with Disabilities Education Improvement Act (IDEIA, 2004) Child Find mandate requires all states to locate and evaluate children suspected of having a disability. Additionally, children suspected of having a disability can be referred for an evaluation by a parent or school personnel. The evaluation is a decision-making process by which a multidisciplinary team determines eligibility for special education and related services. Referrals for evaluations have increased over the years (Lerner & Johns, 2015). Although this is in part due to greater awareness of special education needs, it is also a function of the ambiguity of criteria for determining some eligibility categories and educators' common lack of differentiation between disadvantage and disability.

In order to be considered for a specific learning disability (SLD), for example, IDEIA indicates that a multidisciplinary team must rule out that the primary cause of the academic deficit is caused by a visual, hearing, or motor disability; intellectual disability; emotional disturbance; cultural factors; environmental or economic disadvantages; and/or limited English proficiency (34 C.F.R. § 300.309). In other words, the team must assess whether issues regarding economic disadvantage (e.g., low income, residence in a depressed economic area, inability to afford enrichment materials, receipt of public assistance), environmental disadvantage (e.g., frequent absences, frequent moves, disruption in family structure), and/or cultural differences (e.g., student's cultural background is different from that of most teachers and/or students in the school) constitute the main reason for a student's academic deficiencies rather than an SLD (Greenville Public School District, 2015). A variety of assessment tools (e.g., checklists, question-naires, developmental histories, and interviews with the family) should be used to determine whether a specific learning disability is present (34 C.F.R. § 300.304).

Although federal law authorizes practitioners to consider these so-ciological rule-outs when determining eligibility for SLD, the local edu-cation agency often gives the evaluation team minimal autonomy to use clinical judgment when considering sociological factors. In many cases, the lack of administrative support forces practitioners to disre-gard the extenuating factors that may be contributing to students' poor academic achievement; this, in turn, leads to inappropriately identify-ing some students as having a specific learning disability. This over-sight of exclusionary factors continues to be a barrier in making appropriate referrals for special education and further escalates the overrepresentation of disadvantaged students in special education.

Disproportionate Representation and Socioeconomic Status

A good education is one of the most valuable things a child can re-ceive. It is considered to be a precursor for success, empowerment, and future employment, which ultimately leads to financial stability. Addi-tionally, a good education can also help bridge the gap between social and economic disparities. However, trouble arises when low academic performance that is due primarily to unequal opportunities and low so-cioeconomic status is interpreted as a disability (Harry & Klinger, 2014). Disproportionate representation exists when students' represen-tation in special education significantly exceeds their proportional en-rollment in a school's general population (Blanchett, 2006). Such disproportion suggests that something is awry in the referral, assess-ment, and/or placement process.

Socioeconomic status (SES) "is often measured as a combination of education, income, and occupation" (American Psychological Associa-tion, n.d., p. 1) and is relevant to education. Although low SES affects society as a whole, it has particularly troubling outcomes in children. Children from low SES communities often develop language skills more slowly than their counterparts from high SES communities (APA, n.d.). They also exhibit delayed letter recognition and phonological awareness and are at greater risk for reading difficulties (Aikens & Barbarin, 2008). Overall, they are at risk for academic failure that could lead to them dropping out of school. In fact, the National Center for Education Statistics (2015) reported that in 2012, the high school dropout rate among persons 16–24 years old was highest in low-income families (5.9%), as compared to high-income families (1.3%). Furthermore, Aikens and Barbarin (2008) stated that schools located in low SES communities lack the necessary resources to educate students to the fullest extent, thereby negatively impacting students' academic progress.

Although SES-related factors such as inadequate access to primary and preventive health care, parental unemployment and low wages, parents' irregular work schedules, housing instability, and malnutrition are not the sole determinant of disproportionate representation, these factors do strongly shape cognitive and behavioral outcomes. However, educators often fail to take these environmental factors into account when thinking about a child's academic performance. Inaccurately interpreting low performance as being due to a learning disability, for example, leads to an inappropriate label and referral for special education (Morsy & Rothstein, 2015). Given the mixed outcomes seen in large-scale studies of special education services (Morgan, Frisco, Farkas, & Hibel, 2010; Newman, Wagner, Cameto, & Knokey, 2009) and the potential for stigma and lowered expectations that accompany special education placement, inappropriate placement is likely to lead to further low academic achievement among disadvantaged students.

Subjective referral information and fluctuating eligibility determination procedures that vary from district to district also influence disproportionate representation (Blanchett, 2006). According to Skiba et al. (2006), a common theme among teachers and schools is that they feel unprepared to meet the needs of economically disadvantaged students. Teachers may refer disadvantaged students for an evaluation based on the erroneous belief that special education is the only resource available for helping these struggling learners. Although a percentage of such referrals may represent genuine but misguided efforts to help students, it is also possible that some teachers simply want these "difficult" students out of their classrooms. Given the relatively lower socioeconomic status of many children of color, this means that many disadvantaged students of color will be referred to and placed in special education, even in the absence of a true learning disability or other diagnosis.

Disproportionate Representation Among Students of Color

IDEIA (2004) mandates nondiscriminatory assessment, identification, and placement of individuals with disabilities. This means that students should not be identified as having a disability because of poor achievement due solely to economic and/or environmental disadvantage, cultural factors, linguistic differences, ethnic differences, or racial differences (Coutinho & Oswald, 2004). However, contrary to what federal regulations mandate, students from economic, environmental, and culturally diverse backgrounds are continuously referred for special education and labeled without the consideration of exclusionary factors (National Education Association, 2007). The disproportionate representation of students of color in special education, in particular, has been a persistent problem for more than 40 years (Ford & Russo, 2016; Sullivan, 2011; Zhang & Katsiyannis, 2002). It has been documented at the national level and in many state and local education agencies (Gravois & Rosenfield, 2006). Research has repeatedly shown that being a poor student of color heightens exposure to social risks that compromise academic achievement, eventually leading to a referral for special services (O'Connor & Fernandez, 2006).

Disproportionality is a critical issue, as it suggests discriminatory practices are being upheld in schools. Such unlawful practices are evidence of systematic problems of inequity and marginalization within the education system (Sullivan, 2011). In particular, African American students continue to meet eligibility for special education at a disproportionate rate compared to their Caucasian counterparts (Gravois & Rosenfield, 2006). One of the best known court cases illustrating this disproportionate representation is the case of Larry P. v. Riles (Wade, 1980); African American students were misdiagnosed and wrongly placed in special classes for the "educable mentally retarded" as a result of discriminatory practices and biased intelligence testing. Such unfair methods cause students to receive inadequate education and less-than-optimal outcomes. For example, Wells, Sandefur, and Hogan (2003) examined the immediate post-high school years of adolescents with disabilities and found significant differences between young adults with and without disabilities, with the former group less likely to live independently and less likely to be engaged in employment or additional education.

The U.S. Office for Civil Rights (OCR) monitors overrepresentation of students from racial and ethnic minority groups in special education at the state and local education level. States and school districts must collect and publicly report data on race and ethnicity as these variables relate to the various disability categories assigned to students; the restrictiveness of class and school placements of all students with disabilities; and the incidence, duration, and type of disciplinary actions, including suspensions and expulsions experienced by all students (National Center for Education Statistics, 2013). Where disproportionate representation exists, OCR necessitates systems to implement corrective plans to reduce overrepresentation. In such cases, schools may have to re-examine current referral and policy procedures within their special education program.

Implicit Cultural Bias

In spite of monitoring and efforts to improve the accuracy of placement, disproportionality continues to plague students of color. One possible reason that disproportionality continues to be a problem is because many teachers lack knowledge about various cultures and may interpret students' behaviors through the lens of their own cultural experiences. This can lead to inappropriate referrals for special education that ultimately result in inaccurate identification and placement.

Implicit cultural bias is a strong contributor to racial disproportionality in school discipline and special education placement (Kirwan Institute, 2014). Implicit bias is "the mental process that causes us to have negative feelings and attitudes about people based on characteristics like race, ethnicity, age and appearance" (Kirwin Institute, 2014, p. 3). Implicit biases can be automatically triggered by environmental cues, but they can also be moderated by a variety of factors, such as a person's motives and situational characteristics (Blair, 2002). For example, implicit biases can be overridden by positive (or negative) experiences with a specific person. However, most people—including educators—are generally not aware of their implicit biases; this lack of awareness means that implicit biases have the potential to influence educators' behavior even though they may not realize that this is happening.

The combination of a teaching force largely made up of Caucasian women (U. S. Department of Education, 2016) and a public school student body that is highly diverse (National Center for Education Statistics, 2016) suggests that a cultural mismatch may be contributing to disproportionate representation. Although culturally relevant pedagogy and culturally responsive instruction and classroom management are widely promoted by educational associations (e.g., National Education Association, 2008), these are not always adapted by school systems or individual educators. Without culturally responsive strategies to counter previously held beliefs about students of color, teachers' biases may play into the fear factor many teachers feel in their diverse classrooms (Blair, 2002).

When questioned, educators are the first to indicate that they hold no bias against students or their families. They report believing that all students can succeed. A teacher's ability to help students thrive academically is linked to the teacher's own knowledge, frame of reference when dealing with students of a different ethnicity, and competence in sound pedagogical practices that promote student achievement (Jackson, 2013). Yet, as Cooper (2003) has noted, "teacher effectiveness is . . . connected to educators' deep-seated beliefs about their students' intelligence, character, and potential" (p. 101). One mechanism for the relationship between deep-seated beliefs and teacher effectiveness is expectations for student success. Neal, McCray, Webb-Johnson, and Bridgest (2003) found that teachers were more likely to indicate that students who displayed a "black walking style" needed special education services. Townsend (2000) suggested that "verbal and nonverbal language differences [between students and teachers] may create additional opportunities for cultural conflicts and misinterpretation" (p. 384). These perceptions of students' behavior and communication can shape teachers' expectations, which in turn may result in differential treatment of students of color (and African American male students, in particular), including more negative consequences (Kirwin Institute, 2014). The extreme consequence is repeated office visits, resulting in referrals, dismissal from school, and in some cases, special education labeling (Skiba et al., 2005).

Recent Controversy

Although extensive research has supported the finding that students of color are overrepresented in special education, recent longitudinal research (Morgan et al., 2015) concluded that Hispanic and African American children were consistently *less* likely than otherwise similar Caucasian, English-speaking children to be identified as having a disability. Their findings failed to find any indication that racial-, ethnic-, or language-minority children in the United States are being disproportionately overrepresented in special education, particularly when a variety of confounding variables were controlled for. Instead, results from their data analyses consistently indicated that racial-, ethnic-, and language-minority school children in the United States are *less* likely to be identified as having learning disabilities, speech or language impairments, intellectual disabilities, health impairments, or emotional disturbance.

Furthermore, Morgan and colleagues failed to find a relationship between socioeconomic status and most disability categories. The authors attributed this to the overlap between socioeconomic status and individual academic achievement (which they also included in their analyses). This study has provoked a strong debate about the nature and extent of disproportionate representation among students of color in the special education system. Although Morgan and colleagues presented their findings as evidence that culturally and linguistically diverse students may not be receiving the special education services they need (which is also a social justice issue), the authors and the study have been sharply critiqued on several grounds.

First, Skiba, Artiles, Kozleski, Losen, and Harry (2016) criticized the study's methodology, citing errors due to sampling considerations and the way in which disability status was measured (i.e., through teacher report rather than U.S. Department of Education statistics). Skiba and colleagues (2016) also noted that Morgan et al.'s (2015) use of complex statistical analytical procedures did not necessarily make clear the multidimensional aspects of disproportionality, nor did it advance the theoretical understanding of this predicament. Morgan and Farkas (2016) responded to this critique by noting that they explicitly reported on conflicting explanations and evidence of disproportionate representation, and their analyses allowed for the possibility of either over or underrepresentation. Morgan and Farkas also justified their sampling and measurement strategies and cited similar findings from other large-scale studies of disproportionate representation.

A second critique (Collins, Connor, Ferri, Gallagher, & Samson, 2016) has been made on philosophical and theoretical grounds. Collins and colleagues challenge what they perceive as the underlying assumptions of Morgan et al.'s (2015) work, two of which will be discussed here: that placement in special education is beneficial, and that students are deficient. As noted above, special education identification and placement do not always help students, particularly those who have been labeled with emotional disturbances or intellectual disabilities. Perhaps more importantly, Collins and colleagues (2016) criticize the attribution of overrepresentation to student factors (such as achievement differences) and contextual factors (such as poverty), which they suggest reflects "deficit-based assumptions" (p. 6). Collins and colleagues (2016) note that such assumptions overlook such critical factors as "referral bias, negative stereotypes, lowered expectations, reduced opportunity to learn, or the historical legacies of discrimination" (pp. 6–7). In other words, explanations for disproportionate representation that ignore racial and cultural bias and discrimination are inherently flawed.

In their discussion of disproportionate representation, Sullivan and Proctor (2016) ultimately conclude that ". . . even when racial minority students, and African American students in particular, may demonstrate academic or behavioral deficits, it is difficult to determine whether deficits are attributable to educational disadvantage or disability and whether special education confers the benefits intended" (p. 282). This is the crux of the disproportionate representation problem: It is mediated by multiple factors at both the child level and the institutional level (Skiba et al., 2016). Therefore, school districts need to be vigilant about disproportionality issues and implement effective policies and practices to provide equitable education for all. One key practice is to consider contextual factors that might influence a student's academic performance.

CASE STUDY

Shavonne, a 13-year-old African American eighth grader, was demonstrating poor academic performance. She attended an inner city middle school, nestled in the heart of north Baton Rouge, Louisiana, where the average annual household income was approximately $23,000. Shavonne resided in the same community, in a single parent home, where she was the eldest of three children.

Shavonne's academic deficits in the general education setting were present at the beginning of her eighth grade year. The deficits were first noticed by the general education and special education teachers in her language arts class (teachers were in a co-teaching environment). A review of historical data showed she had difficulty accessing the general education curriculum for the past two years, but there was no indication of a referral for special education. Shavonne struggled with reading comprehension, written expression, and spelling. In addition, she exhibited poor note-taking skills due to her spelling challenges. However, Shavonne had strong math calculation and verbal skills. In the classroom, she seemed sluggish, as she frequently laid her head on the desk. She was inattentive and hardly ever showed an interest in the subject matter. She also appeared to be withdrawn. The general education teacher deemed Shavonne as "lazy" and unmotivated. She was regularly sent out of the general education setting to the office because of her behavior.

When her classroom special education co-teacher asked her why she was so tired every day, Shavonne replied, "Because I don't sleep at night." Further query revealed that Shavonne was functioning in the role of the parent at home. She indicated that her mother worked overnight at a gas station, so she was responsible for taking care of her siblings. At night she would have to scramble to find food for her siblings, find clothes for them to wear to school the next day, and comb her younger sister's hair. She also admitted to everyone sharing a bed, which oftentimes led her to make a pallet on the floor. Every morning she was responsible for making sure she and her siblings were dressed on time and at the bus stop to catch the bus to school, which led her to habitually skip breakfast. Shavonne cited all these reasons for her lethargic demeanor in the classroom. Although the special education co-teacher observed Shavonne to be functioning at a lower level than some of the other children in the class, the special education co-teacher did not see any signs of a learning disability on either formal or informal assessments.

Shavonne participated in high stakes testing (Louisiana Educational Assessment Program [LEAP]) during the spring semester. She scored unsatisfactorily (did not meet expectations) in the areas of English language arts/literacy, science, and social studies. Shavonne was then referred for a special education evaluation through a school building level committee (SBLC) meeting. Despite Shavonne's special education co-teacher's observations, the SBLC wanted her evaluated because they felt she had a learning disability and she was in jeopardy of repeating eighth grade. The SBLC also wanted to ensure that Shavonne would have the proper supports for the upcoming school year. However, the evaluation process was marked by a series of problems. Shavonne's mother did not attend any meetings regarding her daughter's evaluation. The diagnostician never considered Shavonne's environmental conditions as they might have been contributing to her academic performance. Instead, under pressure to label this student, the SBLC concluded that she met the eligibility condition for a specific learning disability.

Shavonne's case is common in academic settings across America in that many children from low SES backgrounds, who do not exhibit threatening, acting-out behaviors, are initially overlooked for academic supports and/or special education referrals. At some point, however, these students' academic difficulties become more apparent or pronounced, and educators are faced with a decision: refer to special education, or attempt to address the issue with enhanced academic supports. Morsy and Rothstein (2015) indicated that parents' irregular work hours, coupled with low wages, can preclude high-quality child care and make it difficult and to create effective home routines. Furthermore, parents of children with low SES backgrounds may themselves be less educated. Because of these factors, children typically have lower test scores and greater emotional and behavioral difficulties. In Shavonne's case, the mere fact that she was deprived of her right to be a "normal child" and forced into the role of matriarch at 13 makes it unsurprising that education was not at the forefront of her mind. Therefore, she struggled in the general education setting. Her poor academic performance and somber manner were more than likely the result of her environmental and economic conditions, not a learning disability. However, sociological factors were not considered, as the desire to have her "labeled" superseded the regular education supports she should have received.

This is a classic case of misdiagnosing children, which ultimately affects their educational outcomes (e.g., Fletcher & Navarrete, 2011). In such situations, the evaluation team has very little independence in exploring other factors that could be contributing to student failure. Instead, they are commanded by administration to test and rely solely on the scores from the assessment instrument to determine eligibility. This may be one reason why the frequency of students identified as having SLD is much higher among those living in poverty (Cortiella & Horowitz, 2014). This system failure continues to be a malignant tumor that aggressively contributes to the overrepresentation of both disadvantaged students and students of color in special education.

DISCUSSION AND RECOMMENDATIONS

Using the Sociological Rule-Out

According to federal regulations, a specific learning disability is "a disorder in one or more of the basic psychological processes involved in understanding or in using language, spoken or written, which may manifest itself in an impaired ability to listen, think, speak, read, write, spell, or do mathematical calculations. . ." (34 C.F.R. § 300.8 (10)(i)). The definition further explains that a specific learning disability "does not include learning problems that are primarily the result of visual, hearing, or motor disabilities, mental retardation, emotional disturbance, *environmental, cultural, or economic disadvantage*" (34 C.F.R. § 300.8 (10)(ii); emphasis added). Evaluators are required to rule out exclusionary factors such as the aforementioned when considering a child for a specific learning disability (Texas Education Agency, 2010).

Best practice suggests that a comprehensive evaluation be conducted by a multidisciplinary team to rule out these factors. The multidisciplinary team consists of a group of qualified professionals representing various disciplines who are responsible for conducting a comprehensive evaluation to determine a student's eligibility for special education services. A comprehensive evaluation requires the use of multiple data sources that include educationally relevant medical findings, standardized tests, informal measures, observations, parent reports, student self-reports, and progress monitoring data from Response to intervention (RTI) approaches (National Joint Committee on Learning Disabilities, 2010). Moreover, it requires data to exclude visual, hearing, or motor disability; cultural factors, environmental, or economic disadvantage; or limited English proficiency (Lerner & Johns, 2015; National Joint Committee on Learning Disabilities, 2010).

In an effort to consider the appropriateness of a special education referral, the multidisciplinary team closely reviews prereferral activities that usually include RTI information. Lerner and Johns (2015) note that the prereferral stage is crucial, as the decision to refer a student for an evaluation has serious consequences. Prereferral activities are highly encouraged to help circumvent a referral for a special education evaluation; once a student is referred, the likelihood is high that the student will meet eligibility for services (Salvia, Ysseldyke, & Bolt, 2007).

However, even in the context of an extensive, multidisciplinary evaluation, such rule-outs can be complicated. For example, research has shown that sociological factors influence brain development and academic achievement (e.g., Hair, Hanson, Wolfe, & Pollak, 2015). Students like Shavonne are challenging to assess because it is difficult to tease apart the relative contributions of poverty, malnutrition, and having to function as an adult because one's parent or guardian is rarely present in the home (Aikens & Barbain, 2008; Geva & Wiener, 2015). The potential role of cultural bias also makes the assessment and diagnostic process more complex. Therefore, a comprehensive evaluation should be based on gathering many sources of data, consulting with other professionals such as a licensed specialist in school psychology (LSSP) to consider social, emotional, and environmental factors, and synthesizing all sources of data to rule out sociological factors in lieu of relying only on test scores. This process makes it less challenging and more plausible to tease apart sociological factors from a true learning disability (LD) by considering sociological and historical data first, and then making an informed decision to proceed with an evaluation for LD or recommend interventions and strategies that focus on socioeconomic inequalities.

It is important to note that the consideration of exclusionary factors does not refute the possibility of a student having a learning disability. Students with learning disabilities may very well also possess characteristics that coincide with what is considered to be an environmental and/or economic disadvantage. However, the goal is to examine such sociological factors as a conceivable cause for low academic performance first, before considering an eligibility condition.

Culturally Responsive Teaching and Curriculum

In addition to formal prereferral interventions, educators need to brainstorm ideas to help close the achievement gap between children from lower socioeconomic backgrounds and those from higher socioeconomic backgrounds. A starting point is the development of culturally responsive teaching and curriculum (e.g., Gay, 2013). Students from diverse backgrounds need highly-qualified, culturally responsive teachers. Educational leaders must pay careful attention to the recruitment and development of teaching staff to ensure that they are culturally aware and engaged. Teachers may benefit from study groups where they review issues that contribute to student failure and focus on cultural awareness and sensitivity. Each group can present information and findings during monthly professional development meetings.

Multicultural educational practices also aid in empowering school culture. Integrating multiculturally-based content into the existing curriculum allows for more ethnically and linguistically diverse learning materials, which can lead to higher levels of student engagement (Zirkel, 2008). This can entail developing a curriculum that incorporates students' cultural backgrounds so that teachers are more aware of challenges disadvantaged students face. Such training can also help support teachers' understanding of the value of students' diverse experiences and viewpoints (Ladson-Billings, 1994).

Involving Families

Best practices indicate that supporting parental involvement within the special education placement process contributes to long-term success of placed students (Center for Parent Information Resources, 2014). Because teachers are primarily trained to provide student-focused services, they may lack formal training in working with families (Mulholland & Blecker, 2008). Culturally relevant training on how to involve families must be specific, results-driven, and monitored consistently.

Parents must be informed of their rights under the Individuals with Disabilities Education Act. However, this informed consent process cannot be reduced to a brief conversation and/or written summary of rights. A dialogue about the special education process that offers time to answer parents' questions and address their concerns is essential. Furthermore, when a special education referral and placement are appropriate, families should have specific interventions to support their involvement in this process. Interventions can focus on logistics (e.g., providing child care during meetings, being flexible in scheduling), communication (e.g., using nontechnical language, providing numerous opportunities to ask questions), and timing and quality of information (e.g., providing parents with assessment reports before meetings to give them time to process the information) (Family Empowerment and Disability Council, 2012).

Advocacy and Outreach

Educators must also become more active with policy making. Helping to devise policies that focus on multicultural issues in an effort to promote equity will help bridge the gap between students from low and high SES backgrounds. One way to start is by providing resources such as books, computers, or tutors to assist students with academic tasks. When students are given supplemental instructional materials, their chances of academic success increase. Another way teachers can help close the achievement gap between students from varying SES levels is to assign students to adult mentors who can provide additional guidance and support. Teachers can also develop an outreach program to gain community support in order to strengthen services for students with economic challenges. Having the community invest in school-based supports that extend beyond the classroom (e.g., after-school enrichment programs, mental health/counseling programs) can increase attendance, improve test scores, and reduce behavioral problems. It is critical to include community members and different agencies when developing policies, as this helps promote awareness of cultural socio-economic issues and increases community buy-in.

Zirkel (2008) reported that empowered school cultures forge strong relationships among students and between students and teachers, which shifts student motivation and boosts achievement. Furthermore, having high expectations for students and making concentrated efforts to engage families are also effective strategies for addressing SES and culture-related academic concerns (Gorsky, 2013). These principles should underlie any efforts to reduce inappropriate referrals to special education and to improve disadvantaged students' outcomes.

The twin issues of disproportionate representation and mistaking disadvantage for disability suggest that educators are not yet fully utilizing various resources to decrease inaccurate referrals. Disproportionality is problematic because it means that some children without disabilities are being placed in special education (Chamberlain, 2005), while other children with disabilities are being denied needed services.

Either scenario represents grave social injustice in education. It is incumbent upon educators to make certain that every child is given a fair chance to receive adequate, appropriate instruction in order to succeed in the academic milieu. It is also imperative that we explore every available option and implement strategies to help students excel in the classroom prior to referring them for an evaluation.

REFERENCES

Aikens, N. L., & Barbarin, O. (2008). Socioeconomic differences in reading trajectories: The contribution of family, neighborhood, and school contexts. *Journal of Educational Psychology, 100*, 235–251.

American Psychological Association. (n.d.). Education and socioeconomic status fact sheet. Retrieved from http://www.apa.org/pi/ses/resources/publications/education.aspx

Blair, I. (2002). The malleability of automatic stereotypes and prejudice. *Personality and Social Psychology Review, 6*, 242–261.

Blanchett, W. J. (2006). Disproportionate representation of African American students in special education: Acknowledging the role of white privilege and racism. *Educational Researcher, 35*(6), 24–28.

Center for Parent Information and Resources. (2014). 10 basic steps in special education. Retrieved from http://www.parentcenterhub.org/repository/steps/

Chamberlain, S. P. (2005). Recognizing and responding to cultural differences in the education of culturally and linguistically diverse learners. *Intervention in School and Clinic, 40*(4), 195–211.

Collins, K. M., Connor, D., Ferri, B., Gallagher, D., & Samson, J. F. (2016). Dangerous assumptions and unspoken limitations: A disability studies in education response to Morgan, Farkas, Hillemeier, Mattison, Maczuga, Li, and Cook (2015). *Multiple Voices for Ethnically Diverse Exceptional Learners, 16*(1), 4–16.

Cooper, C. W. (2003). The detrimental impact of teacher bias: Lessons learned from the standpoint of African American mothers. *Teacher Education Quarterly, 30*(2), 101–116.

Coutinho, M. J., & Oswald, D. P. (2004). Disproportionate representation of culturally and linguistically diverse students in special education: Measuring the problem. Retrieved from http://www.ldonline.org/article/5603/

Family Empowerment and Disability Council. (2012, May). The Individuals with Disabilities Education Act and parent participation. *FEDC Issue Brief*, 1–10.

Fletcher, T. V., & Navarrete, L. A. (2011). Learning disabilities or difference: A critical look at issues associated with the misidentification and placement of Hispanic students in special education programs. *Rural Special Education Quarterly, 30*(1), 30–38.

Ford, D. Y., & Russo, C. J. (2016). Historical and legal overview of special education overrepresentation: Access and equity denied. *Multiple Voices for Ethnically Diverse Exceptional Learners, 16*(1), 50–57.

Gay, G. (2013). Teaching to and through cultural diversity. *Curriculum Inquiry, 43*(1), 48–70.

Geva, E., & Wiener, J. (2015). *Psychological assessment of culturally and linguistically diverse children and adolescents: A practitioner's guide.* New York: Springer.

Gorsky, P. C. (2013). Building a pedagogy of engagement for students in poverty. *Kappan, 95*(1), 48–52.

Gravois, T. A., & Rosenfield, S. A. (2006). Impact of instructional consultation teams on the disproportionate referral and placement of minority students in special education. *Remedial and Special Education, 27*(1), 42–52.

Greenville Public School District. (2015). Environmental/cultural differences and economic disadvantage assessment. Retrieved from http://www.gvillepublic-schooldistrict.com/docs/district/depts/22/environmentcultural%20differences%20and%20economic%20disadvantage%20assessment.pdf

Hair, N. L., Hanson, J. L., Wolfe, B. L., & Pollak, S. D. (2015). Association of child poverty, brain development, and academic achievement. *JAMA Pediatrics, 169*(9), 822–829.

Harry, B., & Klinger, J. (2014). *Why are so many minority students in special education* (2nd ed). New York: Teachers College Press.

Individuals with Disabilities Education Improvement Act of 2004, 34 C.F.R. § 300.4 et seq (Electronic Code of Federal Regulations, 2016).

Jensen, E. (2009). *Teaching with poverty in mind.* Alexandria, VA: Association for Supervision and Curriculum Development.

Lerner, J. W., & Johns, B. H. (2015). *Learning disabilities and related disabilities* (13th ed.). Stamford, CT: Cengage Learning.

Kirwan Institute. (2014). Racial disproportionality in school discipline: Implicit bias is heavily implicated. *Kirwan Institute Brief,* 1–8.

Ladson-Billings. G. (1994). *The dreamkeepers: Successful teaching for African-American students.* San Francisco: Jossey-Bass.

Morgan, P. L., & Farkas, G. (2016). Are we helping all the children that we are supposed to be helping? *Educational Researcher, 45*(3), 226–228.

Morgan, P. L., Frisco, M., Farkas, G., & Hibel, J. (2010). A propensity score matching analysis of the effects of special education services. *Journal of Special Education, 43*(4), 236–254.

Morgan, P. L., Farkas, G., Hillemeier, M. M., Mattison, R., Maczuga, S., Li, H., & Cook, M. (2015). Minorities are disproportionately underrepresented in special education: Longitudinal evidence across five disability conditions. *Education Researcher, 44*(5), 278–292.

Morsy, L., & Rothstein, R. (2015). *Five social disadvantages that depress student performance. Why schools alone can't close achievement gaps.* Economic Policy Institute Report.

Mulholland, R., & Blecker, N. (2008). Parents and special educators: Pre-service teachers' discussion points. *International Journal of Special Education, 23*(1), 49–53.

National Center for Education Statistics. (2015). *Trends in high school dropout and completion rates in the United States: 1972–2012. Retrieved from* http://www.nces.ed.gov/pubs2015/2015015.pdf

National Center for Education Statistics. (2016). *Racial/ethnic enrollment in public schools.* Retrieved from https://nces.ed.gov/programs/coe/indicator_cge.asp

National Education Association. (2007). *Truth in labeling: Disproportionality in special education.* Retrieved from www.nea.org/assets/docs/HE/EW-TruthInLabeling. pdf

National Education Association. (2008). *Promoting educators' cultural competence to better serve culturally diverse students.* Retrieved from http://www.nea.org

National Joint Committee on Learning Disabilities. (2010). Comprehensive assessment and evaluation of students with learning disabilities. *Learning Disability Quarterly, 34*(1), 3–16.

Neal, L. V. I., McCray, A. D., Webb-Johnson, G., & Bridgest, S. T. (2003). The effects of African American movement styles on teachers' perceptions and reactions. *The Journal of Special Education, 37(1), 49–57.*

Newman, L., Wagner, M., Cameto, R., & Knokey, A. M. (2009). *The post-high school outcomes of youth with disabilities up to 4 years after high school: A report from the National Longitudinal Transition Study-2 (NLTS2)* (NCSER 2009–3017). Washington, DC: National Center for Special Education Research.

O'Connor, C., & Fernandez, S. D. (2006). Race, class, and disproportionality: Re-evaluating the relationship between poverty and special education placement. *Educational Researcher, 35*(6), 6–11.

Patten, E., & Krogstad, J. M. (2015). Black child poverty rate holds steady, even as other groups see declines. Retrieved from http://www.pewresearch.org/fact-tank/2015/07/14 black-child-poverty-rate-holds-steady-even-as-other-groups-see-declines/

Salvia, J., Ysseldyke, J., & Bolt, S. (2013). *Assessment in special and inclusive education.* Belmont, CA: Wadsworth/Cengage Learning.

Skiba, R. J., Artiles, A. J., Kozleski, E. B., Losen, D. J., & Harry, E. G. (2016). Risks and consequences of oversimplifying educational inequities: A response to Morgan et al. (2015). *Educational Researcher, 45*(3), 221–225.

Skiba, R. J., Simmons, A., Ritter, S., Kohler, K., Henderson, M., & Wu, T. (2006). The context of minority disproportionality: Practitioner perspectives on special education referral. *Teachers College Record, 108*(7), 1424–1459.

Sullivan, A. L. (2011). Disproportionality in special education identification and placement of English language learners. *Exceptionality Children, 77*(3), 317–334.

Sullivan, A. L., & Proctor, S. (2016). The shield or the sword? Revisiting the debate on racial disproportionality in special education and implications for school psychologists. *School Psychology Forum: Research in Practice, 10*(3), 278–288.

Townsend, B. L. (2000). The disproportionate discipline of African American learners: Reducing school suspensions and expulsions. *Exceptional Children, 66*(3), 381–391.

U.S. Department of Education. (2016). U.S. Department of Education takes action to deliver equity for students with disabilities. Retrieved November 21, 2016, from www.ed.gov/news/press-relases/us-department-education-takes-action-deliver-equity-students-disabilities

Wade, D. L. (1980). Racial discrimination in IQ testing-Larry P. v. Riles. Retrieved from http://vialibrary.depaul.edu/law-review/vol29/iss4/12

Wells, T., Sandefur, G. D., & Hogan, D. P. (2003). What happens after the high school years among young people with disabilities? *Social Forces, 82*(2), 803–832.

Zhang, D., & Katsiyannis, A. (2002). Minority representation in special education. *Remedial and Special Education, 23*(3), 180–187.

Zirkel, S. (2008). The influence of multicultural education practices on student outcomes and intergroup relations. *Teachers College Record, 110*(6), 1147–1181.

Chapter 5

ISSUES IN BILINGUAL ASSESSMENT AND SPECIAL EDUCATION ELIGIBILITY

Griselda Landeros Wells and Brenda De La Garza

INTRODUCTION

English Language Learners (ELLs) are the fastest growing population in the United States. They account for 20 to more than 40 percent of the student population across different states, and it is estimated that by the year 2025, ELLs will account for one out of every four students in the United States (Gandara & Contreras, 2009). Additionally, while English Language Learners are the fastest growing group represented in special education in the United States (Genesee, Lindholm-Leary, Saunders, & Christian, 2005), the federal government did not begin collecting data on special education placement by language status (as opposed to race) until recently. Consequently, studies have found both under- and overrepresentation of ELLs in special education (Sullivan, 2011). While the lack of empirical data makes drawing conclusions about ELLs in special education difficult, what is clear is that ELLs' educational needs are not usually first on the list. Despite the existence of federal legislation and Supreme Court decisions that have mandated equal educational opportunity for ELLs (e.g., Castaneda v. Pickard, 1981; Equal Education Opportunities Act of 1974; Lau v. Nichols, 1974), ELLs remain a high-risk group. The language barrier often results in educators having low expectations, which usually leads to ELLs' placement in lower-level courses and results in segregation and limited educational opportunities (Oakes, 2007). In addition, adolescent ELLs are at particular risk of academic failure, as lack of academic language proficiency in high school is a strong predictor of dropping out or other failure to graduate (Slama, 2012).

One response to ELLs' underachievement has been referral for special education services. Guilberson (2009) found that more than 70% of ELLs referred to special education in one Texas sample were either over- or mis-identified. Sullivan and Bal (2013) found that ELLs were being overidentified in the disability areas of Emotional Disturbance (ED) and Other Health Impairment (OHI), in particular. By placing ELLs in more restrictive environments and segregating them to programs such as special education, educators are excluding these students from general education settings.

A major driving force behind such exclusionary practices is accountability, which has been a focal point in education since it was introduced as part of No Child Left Behind (NCLB) in 2001. The accountability systems that have been set in place push for all students to show progress and to meet a specific standard of achievement (August & Shanahan, 2006). The emphasis on accountability and standardized assessment has resulted in schools doing everything they can in order to keep their funding and to stay open, including the adoption of highly restrictive teaching practices and increased referrals to special education. However, there is no evidence that these strategies have resulted in improved educational outcomes for ELLs; rather, this population continues to fall behind.

BACKGROUND

Disproportionate Representation of ELLs in Special Education

The disproportionate representation of English Language Learners (ELLs) in special education (Linn & Hammer, 2011; Sullivan & Bal, 2013) has been a topic of controversy and discussion among educators and professionals in the field within the past two decades (Artiles, Klingner, & King, 2008). Disproportionate representation refers to "unequal proportions of culturally diverse students in these special [education] programs" (Artiles & Trent, 2013, para. 1). On one end of the disproportionality spectrum, overrepresentation of ELLs is connected to the type or amount of native language support a student is receiving, with ELL students in all-English classrooms five times more likely to be referred to special education than their peers receiving native language support including bilingual and dual language education (Artiles & Ortiz, 2002). Moreover, students who are perceived as having both difficulty acquiring English and a deficiency in their primary language are also often perceived as having a language disability (Klingner, Artiles, & Barletta, 2006). On the other end of the spectrum, underrepresentation of ELLs in special education has also been found, with the size of the ELL population in a school being one determinant of under- vs. overrepresentation (Keller-Allen, 2006). In short, the issue of disproportionality is complex and varies by setting.

Before referring ELLs for a special education evaluation, educators must consider several factors: the students' language acquisition levels, the type of instruction the students are receiving, the types of interventions being used and the progress that the students are making, and cultural factors that may influence the student's learning, such as different views on time management and on how tasks are approached. However, there are several barriers to a careful consideration of these factors, which often lead to educators' difficulty distinguishing between English fluency-related deficits versus learning disabilities (Fletcher & Navarrete, 2003; Klingner & Artiles, 2006; Rinaldi & Samson, 2008). These barriers include the shortage of qualified assessment personnel, problematic methods and tools used during the assessment process, and an over-emphasis on English-only instruction, to the exclusion of evidence-based bilingual practices (Burnette, 2000; Klingner et al., 2006).

Assessment Challenges

The assessment of ELLs poses many challenges for educators (Gonzalez, 2012). According to Mueller (2013), "children who grow up bilingually are not the same as children growing up monolingually" (p. 1). ELLs' development is different depending on their background, language experiences, socioeconomic status, and schooling factors such as teacher training and teacher competence, all of which should be taken into consideration when assessing ELLs' academic abilities. Best practices in the evaluation of ELLs (e.g., Alvarado, 2011) indicate that the evaluator should be bilingual, biliterate, and bicultural. In the absence of such personnel, the use of ancillary examiners or interpreters/translators is acceptable but requires sufficient training of the ancillary/interpreter/translator as well as careful coordination of the assessment (Alvarado, 2011).

Even within school districts that have bilingual evaluators, there are ELLs who have been diagnosed as having a learning or speech disability without the use of proper assessment tools (Mueller, 2013). Not every language represented in U.S. schools has reliable and valid assessment tools. Therefore, in many school systems, assessment personnel often assess ELLs with assessments that have been designed for English monolinguals (Abedi, 2006). Furthermore, many times the assessments used in the school setting are not culturally sensitive. Given the recent development of assessment instruments that are more attuned to children's cultural differences, diagnosticians must be vigilant to use these instruments to ensure cultural fairness.

Professional organizations provide some guidance for increasing the fairness and validity of testing ELLs (e.g., American Educational Research Association, American Psychological Association, and National Council on Measurement in Education, 2014), such as using tests in an appropriate language for the testing purpose, adequate training of interpreters, and establishing reliability and validity of translated tests. However, these general professional assessment standards do not always transfer to concrete recommendations for practice. For example, the standing rules and code of ethics for the National Certification of Educational Diagnosticians (NCED) only outline that diagnosticians "shall not discriminate . . . in the basis of race or ethnicity, gender, age, religion, national origin, sexual orientation, language, socioeconomic or disability status, or any basis prescribed by law" (NCED, 2009, p.12). Although regional guidelines to testing ELLs have been developed (e.g., Alvarado, 2011), no national practice standards exist.

Federal special education guidelines are explicit in their requirement of nondiscriminatory and multidisciplinary assessment (Individuals with Disabilities Education Improvement Act, 2004), which is particularly relevant to the multicultural education of culturally and linguistically diverse students. Appropriate assessment of children who are ELLs sometimes reveals that the problems the child is having are related to language issues, not a learning disability. Language issues not related to a disability can arise from a lack of academic and programming supports that ELLs need in their first language (L1) while they are attempting to learn a second language (L2); without these supports, ELLs will not acquire the foundation needed to fully develop in either language. This can lead to cognitive deficits and mimic a language-learning delay or learning disability, when in reality these children are just not proficient in either language (Roseberry-McKibbin, 2009).

Inadequate Bilingual Programming

Lack of proficiency in either language strongly suggests that ELLs have received inadequate bilingual programming. Hakuta and Gould (1987) suggest that "an ideal bilingual program would aim at fluency in both languages, treating the non-English first language as an asset, rather than as a handicap" (p. 42). Research shows that the ideal language programming–also known as additive bilingualism–entails support and development of the child's L1 along with his or her L2 (Baker, 2011; Thomas & Collier, 2002). Basic interpersonal communication skills, or BICS, which involve cognitively undemanding language, can take up to five years to develop. Cognitive academic language proficiency (cognitively demanding language based on literacy skills), or CALP, can take anywhere from five to seven years to acquire (Cummins, 1981). It is clear that a child functioning at a BICS level has not yet acquired the CALP necessary to be successful in more demanding academic language task requirements–requirements necessary to be a successful learner when English is the primary language of instruction.

Subtractive bilingualism, in which the L1 is not developed and only the L2 is taught, leads to a loss of L1 and subsequent academic failure due to poor skills in both languages (Roseberry-McKibbin, 2009). Students in a subtractive model of bilingual education are faced with a system that significantly reduces their ability to progress from BICS to CALP, and as a result increases the challenges they must overcome in order to reach a level of language proficiency commensurate to their same age peers. Research has found that students more proficient in their native language also have stronger English reading, writing, and oral skills (Genesee, 2006). Students in subtractive models do not develop this crucial native language proficiency. Therefore, proper assessment is crucial in determining if the learning problems a child is experiencing are due to a language issue stemming from a subtractive educational model or to a true disability.

Many teachers, whether in bilingual, ESL, or general education classrooms, truly believe that they support their students by emphasizing and prioritizing English learning to the exclusion of their students' home language. This perspective has been supported by many states' policies, as 30% of ELLs live in states with English-only legislation (Sullivan, 2011). This English-only stance has been in part due to the emphasis that is placed on high scores on standardized assessments (Duffy,

Webb, & Davis, 2009). It is true that when achievement is measured by a one-size-fits-all standardized assessment, many things are overlooked and instructional quality and flexibility suffer in order to reach the standards that have been set.

For example, "in order to raise test scores, more and more schools demand fidelity to program designs and require teacher candidates to teach with highly prescriptive materials" (Duffy et al., 2009, p. 189). Professionalism has been forgotten and educators' learning has been overshadowed by the expectations set by the system. Furthermore, the use of prescriptive curriculum and the high emphasis on standardized assessments affects students who cannot "keep up" with such rigid teaching practices. Even when teachers recognize that the use of their students' language and culture as part of their instruction is important, which August and Shanahan (2010) found to be particularly true for ELLs, teachers usually go back to using what the school district or school has imposed. These teaching practices also push the use of the English language as the sole or most important language to learn and use at school.

Smith, Jimenez, and Martinez-Leon (2003) argue that "expecting children from other countries to flourish under approaches based on only U.S. mainstream cultures is naïve, unjust, and ultimately unproductive" (p. 780). One underlying tenet of this expectation appears to be the belief that speaking a different language is a "problem," which is a misconception among some teachers (Lee & Oxelson, 2006). Such English-only attitudes have spread over many school districts across the United States, resulting in an unwritten English-only rule even though they claim to have bilingual or ESL programs. Valenzuela (2009) argues that this practice tends to subtract students' identity and culture and attempts to supplant it with the dominant culture's identity. It is this subtractive approach that, according to Darder (2013), "can cause students to experience a sense of isolation, frustration and disconnection" (p. 27) impacting their "sense of belonging in the world" (Darder, 2013, p. 26). The students' context has to be taken into consideration as part of their academic development and progress. When speaking a different language is seen as a problem and not as a resource, educators embrace a deficit view of the ELLs in their classrooms. This in turn affects their teaching and the relationships that they build with their students (Valenzuela, 2009).

In our globalized society, it is disappointing that bilingualism and multilingualism are seen as inferior in the United States when so many other countries value and treasure their language diversity. This is not to say that bilingualism and multilingualism do not exist in the United States, but as Gort and Bauer (2012) state, this often times happens "in spite of an educational system that has little understanding of the linguistic and cultural resources they possess" (p. 1). Gort and Bauer (2012) are here referring to the children who, even when going into systems in which bilingualism is not appreciated, still develop bilingual and biliterate skills.

Differences between ELL and Special Education Programming

In the face of inadequate assessment tools and practices and an educational system that contributes to ELLs' language difficulties, it is no wonder that ELLs are overrepresented in special education services. Some might argue that special education services benefit ELLs who are slower to develop language proficiency, given the additional funding that is spent on students in special education. However, this is not the case. Many times, ELLs are taught strategies used for struggling learners; while these strategies are helpful to some degree, ELL students require specialized strategies for teaching English and reading to bilingual students. Qualifying ELLs as having disabilities in order to provide them access to additional resources is not only misguided, it also delves into the unethical. Special education teachers are rarely specialists in bilingual education and therefore do not have the expertise in programming for ELLs' specific needs. If ELL students do have an underlying disability, then these students should be provided with dual programming services (i.e., both bilingual and special education). "When ELLs are identified as having disabilities, their need for instruction in English language development does not end. . . . ELLs with disabilities need the services entitled to students with disabilities as well as the services designed to support ELLs" (Figueroa, Klinger, & Baca, 2013, p. 9).

The language difficulties of many children who are culturally and linguistically diverse could be avoided with proper programming that incorporates principles of second language acquisition. Rather than simply leading a child into a difficult situation by ignoring language learning research, educators should consistently apply these principles into the programming of these children in order to offer them better opportunities for success. If, on the other hand, a child has already been exposed to inadequate language programming, then it is imperative for educators to consider this when determining the cause of the child's language difficulties.

CASE STUDY

Sonia was a Hispanic student in seventh grade who had received instruction in public schools in the U.S. since prekindergarten. She was identified as a Limited English Proficient (LEP) student and was struggling academically. Sonia's parents spoke only Spanish, as did her grandparents who also lived in the home. A review of sociological factors indicates that Sonia was identified as an "at-risk" student and was eligible for free school lunch. This "at-risk" label can encompass numerous students with an array of factors that could cause them to be at risk of dropping out of school. According to the Texas Education Agency (2015), one of these factors is a student identified as being Limited English Proficient or LEP. The student in this case study not only met the LEP status "at-risk" factor, but other factors as well. As shown in Table 5.1, Sonia had numerous characteristics of a student who is at risk for dropping out of school (The Center for Public Education, 2007).

Sonia's background indicates numerous obstacles outside of the school setting that could affect her school outcomes. Her family's low socioeconomic status put her at a disadvantage in terms of school success. The family's limited monetary funds paired with a lack of ability to help their child with homework and school projects due to language barriers placed Sonia at risk for poor school attainment.

A bilingual psychoeducational evaluation was conducted for Sonia after her school's Response to Intervention (RTI) team determined an assessment for special education eligibility for a learning disability was appropriate. This evaluation indicated that she was a nonbalanced bilingual with no clear language dominance. Her vocabulary was better developed in Spanish, but her reasoning skills were slightly higher in English. Achievement testing results indicated higher scores in Spanish despite English instruction that began in prekindergarten, where she was quickly transitioned into an all-English classroom, continued with English as a Second Language (ESL) strategies, and finally received

Table 5.1
DROP-OUT FACTORS AND CHARACTERISTICS
OF CASE STUDY STUDENT

Possible future drop-out factors	*Sonia's risk factors*
Demographic Background:	
• poverty • certain minority groups • male students • limited English proficiency • learning or emotional disabilities • high family mobility • over-age for their grade level	• Hispanic • LEP • Living in poverty range • 3 out of 7 factors present
Family factors:	
• Single-parent homes • Mother was a high school drop-out • Family provides limited support for learning • Older siblings who were drop-outs	• Sonia's parents did not finish high school in their native country of Mexico. • Although supportive, their lack of the English language limited their ability to help her with homework and school projects. • 2 out of 4 factors present
Adult Responsibilities:	
• Teenage parents • Teenage marriage • Job responsibilities (depending on gender, job type, work hours per week)	• Sonia did not have any of the risk factors in this category. • 0 out of 3 factors present
Educational Experiences:	
• Struggle academically • Behind in course credits • Retention • Absenteeism/truancy • Poor school behavior • Limited participation in extracurricular activities • Poor interpersonal relationships with teachers and peers	• Academic difficulties • Limited participation in extracurricular activities (due to lack of transportation and lack funds associated with participation in some of these activities) • 2 out of 7 factors present
Risk factors: 21	**7 out of 21 risk factors present for Sonia**

exclusively English instruction. She displayed an average cognitive ability profile when tested in her native language.

Although this student participated in an RTI program, data suggested that this program did not apply scientific, research-based, tiered interventions with integrity and fidelity. There was also limited progress monitoring conducted during the RTI process; therefore, only minimal changes to programming were recommended and made. These circumstances, paired with psychoeducational assessment findings that no pattern of strengths and weaknesses was present (Sonia's school district used this approach to determine LD eligibility), made it difficult for the evaluator to rule out her Limited English Proficiency (one of the several exclusionary factors) as the chief cause of her academic difficulties. Other exclusionary factors that also influence this case were cultural factors and environmental or economic disadvantage factors.

Based on all information and assessment results, Sonia was found not eligible for special education as a student with a Learning Disability because it was determined that her difficulties with language were due to second language learner issues and not a disability. An additive bilingual model would have maintained Sonia's native language and enriched her second language, leading to proficiency in both languages (Thomas & Collier, 2002); however, Sonia's school district adopted a subtractive bilingual program in which assimilation into the second language is the goal, with monolingualism being the final outcome. This subtractive programming establishes a lack of value for the student's first language, as the aim is to do away with it.

Although considered a LEP student, Sonia was in a school district that applies bilingual programming methods in which students, after being in bilingual classes, are quickly transitioned into all-English instruction. Although Sonia has been in the same school district since prekindergarten, she has continued to struggle academically despite average intellectual ability. The unfounded belief that in order to succeed, all students, regardless of their specific needs and circumstances, must become English speakers as soon as possible after entering the school system, has failed Sonia. Uniformity for all and the hope that special education could somehow help her succeed were not the answers for this child.

Despite not meeting criteria for special education services, the fact that she was assessed has actually helped her. Assessment personnel involved in her evaluation, being trained in identifying ELLs with disabilities and with background in disproportionality, were able to develop a suitable RTI plan that incorporates strategies specific for addressing the needs of struggling ELLs. Her teachers were also provided information on second language acquisition and specifically how BICS and CALP affect ELLs and their programming. Sonia is currently provided an RTI plan that includes interventions rich in phonological awareness activities in her native language, which will help her develop sound/symbol relationships in her second language in order to increase reading performance. She now receives targeted instruction in vocabulary recognition to help her decipher English vocabulary by using her knowledge of the Spanish language, which shares many cognates with English (Alvarado, 2011). Oral proficiency in her native language is also being more fully developed in order to help with language transfer between her first and second language, as this has been shown to facilitate the development of language and literacy in English (National Reading Panel, 2000). The goal is to develop her reading ability in Spanish in order to increase her English reading and comprehension skills, which will in turn help increase her overall skills in her current academic setting.

DISCUSSION AND RECOMMENDATIONS

Sonia resides in an area of South Texas that is predominantly Hispanic, where Spanish is spoken in abundance. The population of Texas in 2015 was 38.8% Hispanic (U.S. Census Bureau, 2015), with the Lower Rio Grande Valley (where Sonia lives) having a 90% Hispanic population (FSG, 2011). However, Texas is not alone in facing the task of providing English Language Learners an education. Between 2004 and 2012, the number of ELLs increased over 100% in the states of Kansas, Louisiana, Massachusetts, Maryland, Michigan, South Carolina, and West Virginia (Office of English Language Acquisition, 2015); these states now face the challenges of providing educational services to ELLs, previously only well known to states such as California, New Mexico, Arizona, Florida, and Texas, among others. Spanish ranked as the most commonly spoken second language in the United States, followed by Chinese, Vietnamese, Arabic, and Hmong. Spanish speakers encompassed 3,562,860 students during the 2011-2012 school year, followed by 88,798 Chinese speakers during that same time (OELA, 2015). The majority of these students (57%) were born in the United Sates, and 37% were considered nonnative English speakers due to having at least one parent who was foreign-born and therefore having a language other than English as their first language.

These students are becoming known as "long-term" English learners because, despite being enrolled in U.S. schools for five or more years, they are not meeting exit criteria from ELL status (OELA, 2015). Clearly, the education of ELLs is increasing and will likely continue to increase exponentially, as was the case when schools in Maryland experienced an over 200% increase in their ELL population during the 2011–2012 school year (OELA, 2015). Our educational system in the United States must reconsider current practices in bilingual education and transform its view of ELLs, beginning with a critical examination of subtractive practices that de-emphasize a learner's first language. Until this happens, ELLs will continue to underachieve and be mistakenly diverted to special education.

Dual Language Programming

Although legislation is currently in place to support English Language Learners, changes are needed in order to ensure programming that is consistent with research indicative of successful outcomes. For example, Title VI of the Civil Rights Act of 1964 mandates that schools "must take affirmative steps to ensure that students with limited English proficiency (LEP) can meaningfully participate in their educational programs and services" (U.S. Department of Justice and U.S. Department of Education, 2015, p. 1). The Act indicates that ELL programming should be "educationally sound in theory and effective in practice" (U.S., Department of Justice and U.S. Department of Education, 2015, p. 12). However, guidance from the U.S. Department of Education describes four vastly different types of ELL programming, ranging from Structured English Immersion (a subtractive approach) to Dual Language (an additive approach). While all four programs may be theoretically sound, they are not equal in effectiveness; this provides a "loophole" for schools to use less costly but less effective programming.

Fortunately, the existence of dual language programs in the United States is slowly growing. There has been a rise in dual language programs across the United States in cities such as Boston, Los Angeles, North Carolina, the District of Columbia, and New York City. In 2000 there were less than 300 of these dual language programs nationwide; by 2011 it was estimated that the number had reached 2,000. According to recent research, during the 2012–2013 school year, 39 states offered dual language programming (OELA, 2015). While Spanish was prevalent among these programs, other languages such as Chinese were also offered (Gross, 2016). A 12-year study by Umansky, Valentino, and Reardon (2016) found that in the long term, "two-language programs generally benefit ELLs as much as or more than English immersion programs across academic, English proficiency" (p. 16). They go on to state that while in some cases the outcomes were minimal, in others the benefits were "quite large" (p. 16). By increasing ELLs' CALP, dual language programs can help decrease overidentification of ELLs in special education.

Response to Intervention

To further reduce overidentification of ELLs in special education, efforts should be made to provide targeted interventions for these students. Response to Intervention (RTI) programs that target not only academics but also students' cultural and linguistic needs must be considered before referring an ELL for special education evaluation. Taking into account students' differences when coordinating and planning for instruction is key (Garcia & Ortiz, 2006). It is important for educators to understand that in order to build the background knowledge needed to learn and understand what is being taught, the students' culture and language must be taken into consideration. Whatever ELLs, and all students, bring from home should be valued and act as a driving force for the curriculum being taught in our schools. Therefore, involving students' families as part of the educational process should be a priority. Parents should be seen as a resource, and educators should work in building relationships with the parents as well as the students (Garcia & Ortiz, 2006; Valenzuela, 2009).

In conjunction with RTI, the prereferral process is of utmost importance in the proper identification of ELLs with disabilities. An appropriate prereferral process could facilitate the decision of the multidisciplinary team (MDT) in helping them distinguish between actual disabilities and sociocultural differences (Wilkinson, Ortiz, Robertson,

& Kushner, 2006). It is important that ELLs are exposed to "positive and effective learning environments that are culturally and linguistically responsive" (Liasidou, 2013, p. 13). The prereferral process should include methods by which a student's language needs are addressed using a variety of strategies during instruction. ELLs need explicit instruction in language and vocabulary and multiple opportunities to use academic language (Dutro & Kinsella, 2010) in addition to the use of visuals to support their learning (Sandford, Brown, & Turner, 2012). Additionally, any interventions and assessments used during the prereferral process should take into consideration the student's language proficiency and level of acculturation.

Changing the System

Current knowledge of language acquisition (BICS/CALP) and effective bilingual programming (maintenance bilingual programming resulting in additive bilingualism) must be implemented in order to create successful bilingual students rather than producing English monolinguals with lost prospects and reduced marketability in an ever growing global society. Educators, especially teachers, are an important part of creating educational environments that accept and value students' language and culture. Increasing teachers' knowledge of the most appropriate and successful programming for bilingual students is essential. Teacher preparation programs should include bilingual education classes for all general education teacher candidates. In particular, there must be an emphasis on the importance of gaining knowledge in the concepts of BICS and CALP in addition to coursework that supports research on the most effective bilingual programming and not simply an overview of different bilingual models.

Increased education in cultural competence must also be integrated into teacher training. When teachers spend time with their students and make an effort to get to know their lives, they are able to create relationships that may translate into students learning (Valenzuela, 2009). Soltero-Gonzalez (2009) encouraged the creation of "spaces where children learn how to draw on their linguistic strengths" (p. 288). Such spaces will facilitate efforts to determine whether a child needs ELL and/or special education services. When special education services are truly needed, they must be implemented with integrity, fidelity, and attention to any language issues that may be interacting with a disability.

School systems are creating students who are proficient neither in their first language nor in their second language, leaving many without the opportunity to reach their academic potential and incorrectly placing many into special education programs that do little to help them. Simply placing these students in special education does not solve the problem of low proficiency and academic underachievement. In contrast, using the students' native language as a resource can help ELLs learn and strengthen their English proficiency while not losing themselves in a new language and culture (Baker, 2011). Additionally, increasing native language support and dual language programming can ensure that students are able to overcome issues related to language deficiency, which may have otherwise mistakenly landed them in special education programs. Given that the ELL population is growing faster than any other group in the United States, and knowing that the underachievement of this population may lead to an economic downfall, educational policy must prioritize bilingual programs that support students' identities and meet their needs, whether they have a disability or not.

REFERENCES

Abedi, J. (2006). Psychometric issues in the ELL assessment and special education eligibility. *Teachers College Record, 108*(11), 2282–2303.

Alvarado, C. G. (2011). Best practices in the special education evaluation of students who are culturally and linguistically diverse. Retrieved from http://www.educationeval.com/yahoo_site_admin/assets/docs/Best_Practices_2011.11182801.pdf

American Educational Research Association, American Psychological Association, & National Council on Measurement in Education. (2014). *Standards for educational and psychological testing*. Washington, DC: American Educational Research Association.

Artiles, A., Klingner, J., & King, K. (2008). Bilingual special education. In J. M. González (Ed.), *Encyclopedia of bilingual education in the United States* (pp. 88–92). London: Sage.

Artiles, A., & Ortiz, A. (2002). *English language learners with special needs*. Washington, D.C.: Center for Applied Linguistics.

Artiles, A. J., & Trent, S. O. (2013). Culturally/Linguistically diverse students, representation of. In C. R. Reynolds, K. J. Vannest & E. Fletcher-Janzen (Eds.), *Encyclopedia of special education: A reference for the education of children, adolescents, and adults with disabilities and other exceptional individuals*. Hoboken, NJ: Wiley. Retrieved from http://ezproxy.stthom.edu:2048/login?qurl=http%3A%2F%2Fsearch.credoreference.com%2Fcontent%2Fentry%2Fwileyse%2Fculturally_linguistically_diverse_students_representation_of%2F0

August, D., & Shanahan, T. (2006). *Developing literacy in second-language learners: Report of the National Literacy Panel on Language-Minority Children and Youth.* Mahwah, NJ: Lawrence Erlbaum.

August, D., & Shanahan, T. (2010). Response to a review and update on developing literacy in second-language learners: Report of the National Literacy Panel on Language Minority Children and Youth. *Journal of Literacy Research, 42,* 341–348.

Baker, C. (2011). *Foundations of bilingual education and bilingualism.* Bristol, UK: Multilingual Matters.

Burnette, J. (2000). Assessment of culturally and linguistically diverse students for special education eligibility (ERIC EC Digest #E604). Arlington, VA: ERIC Clearinghouse on Disabilities and Gifted Education.

Castaneda v. Pickard, 648 F.2d 989 (5th Cir. 1981).

Center for Public Education. (2007). Keeping kids in school: What research tells us about preventing dropouts. Retrieved from http://www.centerforpubliceducation.org/Main-Menu/Staffingstudents/Keeping-kids-in-school-At-a-glance/Keeping-kids-in-school-Preventing-dropouts.html

Cummins, J. (1981). Empirical and theoretical underpinnings of bilingual education. *Journal of Education, 163*(1), 16–29.

Darder, A. (2013). Rewriting the world: literacy, Inequality and the brain. *The New England Reading Association Journal, 49*(1), 22–32

Duffy, G., Webb, S. & Davis S. (2009). Literacy education at a crossroad. In J. Hofmann & Y. Goodman (Eds.), *Changing literacies for changing times* (pp. 189–197). NY: Routledge.

Dutro, S., & Kinsella, K. (2010). English language development: Issues and implementation at grades 6–12. In California State Department of Education (Ed.), *Improving education for English learners: Research-based approaches* (pp. 151–207). Sacramento, CA: California Department of Education.

Equal Education Opportunities Act of 1974, 20 U.S.C. §1203(f) (1974).

Figueroa, R., Klingner, J., & Baca, L. (2013, Winter/Spring). The present and future of bilingual/ESL special education. In K. Liu, E. Watkins, D. Pompa, P. McLeod, J. Elliott & V. Gaylord (Eds). *Impact: Feature issue on educating K-12 English language learners with disabilities, 26*(1). Minneapolis, MN: University of Minnesota, Institute on Community Integration.

Fletcher, T. V. & Navarrete, L. A. (2003). Learning disabilities or difference: A critical look at issues associated with the misidentification and placement of Hispanic student in special education programs. *Rural Special Education Quarterly, 22,* 37–40.

FSG. (2011). South Texas regional overview. Retrieved from http://greatertexasfoundation.org/wp-content/uploads/2011/03/South-Texas-Full-Research-Loop-FINAL.pdf

Gándara, P., & Contreras, F. (2009). *The Latino education crisis: The consequences of failed social policies.* Cambridge, MA: Harvard Education Press.

Garcia, S. B., & Ortiz, A. A. (2006). Preventing disproportionate representation: Culturally and linguistically responsive prereferral interventions. *Teaching Exceptional Children, 38*(4), 64–68.

Genesee, F. (2006). *Educating English language learners: A synthesis of research evidence.* Cambridge University Press.

Genesee, F., Lindholm-Leary, K. J., Saunders, W., & Christian, D. (2005). English language learners in U.S. schools: An overview of research findings. *Journal of Education for Students Placed at Risk, 10*(4), 363–385.

Gonzalez, V. (2012). Assessment of bilingual/multicultural Pre-K–Grade 12 students: A critical discussion of past, present, and future issues. *Theory into Practice, 51,* 290–296.

Gort, M., & Bauer, E. B. (2012). Introduction. Holistic approaches to bilingual/biliteracy development, instruction and research. In E. B. Bauer & M. Gort (Eds.), *Early biliteracy development* (pp. 1–7). New York: Routledge.

Gross, N. (2016, August 3). Dual-language programs on the rise across the U.S. Education Writers Association. Retrieved from http://www.ewa.org/blog-latino-ed-beat/dual-language-programs-rise-across-us

Hakuta, K., & Gould, L. J. (1987). Synthesis of research on bilingual education. *Educational Leadership, 44(6)*, 38–45.

Individuals with Disabilities Education Improvement Act of 2004, 34 C.F.R. § 300.8 (Electronic Code of Federal Regulations, 2016).

Keller-Allen, C. (2006). *English language learners with disabilities: Identification and other state policies and issues.* Project Forum of the National Association of State Directors of Special Education.

Kligner, J., & Artiles, A. (2006). English language learners struggling to read: Emergent scholarship on linguistic differences and learning disabilities. *Journal of Learning Disabilities, 39*, 386–389.

Klingner, J. K., Artiles, A. J., & Barletta, L. M. (2006). English language learners who struggle with reading: Language acquisition or LD? *Journal of Learning Disabilities, 39*, 108–128.

Lau v. Nichols, 414 U.S. 563 (1974).

Lee, J.S. & Oxelson, E. (2006). "It's not my job": K-12 teacher attitudes toward students' heritage language maintenance. *Bilingual Research Journal, 30,* 453–477.

Liasidou, A. (2013). Bilingual and special education needs in inclusive classrooms: Some critical and pedagogical considerations. *Support for Learning, 28*(1), 11–16.

Linn, D., & Hammer, L. (2011). English language learner disproportionality in special education: Implications for the scholar-practitioner. *Journal of Educational Research and Practice, 1*(1), 70–80.

Mueller Gathercole, V. C. (2013). Assessment of bilinguals: Innovative solutions. In V. C. Mueller Gathercole (Ed.), *Solutions for the assessment of bilinguals* (pp. 1–9). Bristol, UK: Multilingual Matters.

National Certification of Educational Diagnosticians. (2009). *Nationally Certified Educational Diagnostician Program Code of Ethics.* Retrieved from http://www.ncedb.org/pdfs/ncedethics.pdf

National Reading Panel. (2000). T*eaching children to read: An evidence-based assessment of the scientific research literature on reading and its implications for reading instruction.* Washington, DC: National Institute of Child Health and Human Development.

No Child Left Behind Act of 2001, Pub. L. No. 107–110. 115 Stat. 1425 (2001).

Oakes, J. (2007). Limiting students' school success and life chances: The impact of tracking. In A. C. Ornstein, E. F. Pajak & S. B. Ornstein (Eds.), *Contemporary issues in curriculum* (pp. 208–124). Boston: Pearson.

Office of English Language Acquisition. (2015). *Fast facts: Profiles of English learners (ELs)*. U.S. Department of Education. Retrieved from https://www2.ed.gov/about/offices/list/oela/fast-facts/pel.pdf

Rinaldi, C., & Samson, J. (2008). English language learners and response to intervention: Referral considerations. *TEACHING Exceptional Children, 40*(5), 6–14.

Roseberry-McKibbin, C. (2009, September). *Differentiating language differences from language learning disabilities: Practical strategies.* Invited presentation, Texas Region One ESC, Edinburg, TX.

Sanford, A. K., Brown, J., & Turner, M. (2012). Enhancing instruction for English learners in Response to Intervention systems: The PLUSS Model. *Multiple Voices for Ethnically Diverse Exceptional Learners, 13*(1), 56–70.

Slama, R. B. (2012). A longitudinal analysis of academic English proficiency outcomes for adolescent English language learners in the United States. *Journal of Educational Psychology, 104*(2), 265–285.

Smith, P. H., Jimenez, R. T., & Martinez-Leon, N. (2003). Other countries' illiteracies: What U.S. educators can learn from Mexican schools. *The Reading Teacher, 56*(8), 772–781.

Soltero-Gonzalez, L. (2009). Preschool Latino immigrant children: Using the home language as a resource for literacy learning. *Theory Into Practice, 48*(4), 283–289.

Sullivan, A. L. (2011). Disproportionality in special education identification and placement of English language learners. *Exceptional Children, 77*, 317–334.

Sullivan, A. L., & Bal, A. (2013). Disproportionality in special education: Effects of individual and school variables on disability risk. *Exceptional Children, 79*, 475–494.

Texas Education Agency. (2015). Texas academic performance report glossary (pp. 4–5). Retrieved from https://rptsvr1.tea.texas.gov/perfreport//tapr/2015/glossary.pdf

Thomas, W., & Collier, V. (2002). *A national study of school effectiveness for language minority students' long-term academic achievement.* Santa Cruz, CA and Washington, DC: Center for Research on Education, Diversity & Excellence

Umansky, I. M., Valentino, R. A., & Reardon, S. F. (2016). The promise of two-language education: A 12-year study compares how English language learners fare in English immersion, bilingual, and dual immersion programs. *Educational Leadership, 73*(5), 10-17.

U.S. Census Bureau. (2015). Quick facts: Texas. Retrieved from http://www.census.gov/quickfacts/table/PST045216/48

U.S. Department of Justice and U.S. Department of Education. (2015). Dear colleague letter on English learner students and limited English proficient parents. Retrieved from https://www2.ed.gov/about/offices/list/ocr/letters/colleague-el-201501.pdf

Valenzuela, A. (2009). Subtractive schooling, caring relations, and social capital in the schooling of U.S.-Mexican youth. In D. J. Flinders & S. J. Thornton (Eds.), *The curriculum studies reader* (3rd ed., pp. 336–347). New York: Routledge.

Wilkinson, C., Ortiz, A., Robertson, P., & Kushner, M. (2006). English language learners with reading-related LD: Linking data from multiple sources to make eligibility determinations. *Journal of Learning Disabilities, 39*(2), 129–142.

Chapter 6

FALLING THROUGH THE CRACKS: TWO CASES OF INDIVIDUALIZED EDUCATION PROGRAMS GONE AWRY

CORRIE STANISZEWSKI

INTRODUCTION

Across school districts in America, children in special education are currently being educated based on Individualized Education Programs (IEPs). An IEP is a document created by a team of professionals involved in the child's education and includes specific goals that are supposed to ensure a steady stream of progress throughout the child's entire education. These plans are supposed to be tailored to children's individual needs, allowing them to progress to their maximum educational capability. There are legal requirements set forth by the Individuals with Disabilities Education Improvement Act (IDEIA, 2004) that must be addressed within IEPs. Additional requirements were introduced with the No Child Left Behind Act of 2001. While implementation of all the requirements stated by these two pieces of legislation is critical for compliance with federal standards, the most critical component in terms of educational movement forward is the formulation and implementation of appropriate IEP objectives.

IEP objectives are goals designed to ensure progress through demonstration of movement towards mastery levels. IEP objectives are supposed to take into account each child's learning needs in an effort to provide an appropriate education, regardless of ability. When special education laws were first put into effect, they mandated that children with special needs be tested and educated to the best of their ability. The decision of how to implement these new laws was left to the states

(Martin, Martin, & Terman, 1996). However, now this system is so regulated that too much focus is spent on being procedurally compliant (Christle & Yell, 2010) versus providing truly individualized education geared towards creating successful adults able to participate within their community as independently as possible. Certain federal regulations, more specifically the requirement for all academic IEP goals to be tied to grade-level objectives, have ended up harming students in a variety of ways. While the mere formation of special education is an achievement of social justice on its own, based on the experiences and outcomes of those being serviced in special education, additional reform is needed (Connor, 2014).

BACKGROUND

IEP Formulation: The Effects of IDEA

Beginning in 1975, the creation of IEPs was outlined in the Education for All Handicapped Children Act (EAHC, 1975) as a way to ensure that students with disabilities receive a free appropriate public education (FAPE). Over time, the subsequent education laws (IDEA in 1990, 1997, and 2004) have updated requirements in attempts to continue to improve outcomes. Currently, an IEP is to be created by a school-based team with specified team members: minimally, the student (if appropriate), the student's parent, at least one of the student's teachers from general education, at least one of the student's teachers from special education, a representative of the local education agency, and a specialist who can interpret assessment results (Christle & Yell, 2010). In addition to IEPs being devised by the team members listed, legislation also stipulates that IEPs must address specific components. Christle and Yell (2010) outlined the eight components required to achieve procedural compliance:

1. IEPs must contain a statement of present levels of performance, which must address both academic and functional strengths and weaknesses.
2. IEPs must contain objectives that are measurable.
3. IEPs must have a defined method for collecting and reporting individual progress.
4. IEPs must outline provision of special education and related services.
5. IEPs must specify the degree to which a child will not participate in the general education setting.

6. IEPs must state student participation in assessments, both statewide and district.
7. IEPs must summarize transition services by the time the student is 16 years old.
8. IEPs must contain frequency of services, location of services and duration of services, as well as a given start date. (p. 110)

While these components must be addressed within the IEP, the overall goal of the IEP continues to be the provision of FAPE so that all students in special education programs have the opportunity to achieve optimal outcomes.

Under the 2004 revision, IDEA added an additional stipulation that special education, related services, and supplementary aids and services must be based on peer-reviewed research (PRR) when such methods are available (Yell, Katsiyannis, Losinski, & Marshall. 2016). The language of "extent practicable" (IDEA, as cited in Yell et al., 2016, p. 253) has been debatable since the inclusion of this new requirement, and in 2006 it was clarified that while recommended, PRR was not required in order to ensure FAPE. Furthermore, over the course of multiple lawsuits, it has been further clarified that not even the methods found to be optimal by PRR must be implemented in order to ensure FAPE (Etscheidt & Curran, 2010). Despite the seeming flexibility of this new requirement, it adds the additional necessity that teachers and staff implementing IEPs must be cognizant of the most current methodologies related to the IEPs they create, and be able to weigh the effectiveness of not only those methodologies, but also any other methodologies considered (Yell et al., 2010). However, the final decision when it comes to which methods to use in implementing a student's IEP should always strive for the ultimate goal of ensuring the child is educated to his or her fullest potential.

Recent reviews of the application of these requirements, especially related to goal formulation and presentation, found discrepancies between procedural compliance and substantive compliance (Christle & Yell, 2010). While schools were able to demonstrate procedural compliance through creation of IEP plans that addressed all the components required by IDEA, their ability to demonstrate substantive compliance through actual execution of such plans fell short. The top issues that lead to substantive noncompliance were lack of teacher training in IEP development, lack of effective team processes, inability to effectively implement IEP plans, and excessive demands on teacher time (Christle & Yell, 2010). This sentiment was echoed by Etscheidt and Curran (2010), who found that many teachers simply do not understand how to merge appropriate methodology with the requirements set forth in the student's IEP.

Etscheidt and Curran (2010) made suggestions to improve these issues and increase the effectiveness of the school-based teams charged with creating appropriate IEPs. A baseline should be established through careful assessment, along with a determination of strengths and weaknesses related to the student's present levels of performance in academic and functional areas. The team should then develop both academic and functional goals in order to meet the needs of the students. This has been further expanded upon by suggesting that the school-based team should focus more on utilization of the student's strengths versus remediation of weaknesses (Weishaar, 2010). After creating suitable goals, the school-based team should then decide educational placement that would be most appropriate in order to achieve the goals set forth. More specifically, the team must consider how much time is needed in special education, how much time is needed in general education, and what related services and supplementary aids are required, all while considering how to put these goals into action using techniques supported by PRR.

As the discussion of IEP formulation is presented, the issue of IEP objectives is constantly at the forefront. The components of appropriate IEPs are well-known by the public school system. However, how to apply those components has been where the problem largely lies. How to determine appropriate educational goals and how to present them within a structured curriculum in order for a student to reach his or her ideal educational and functional capability is not well defined. As a result, commonly observed problems include teacher inability to implement IEP objectives within the curriculum, creation of IEP objectives that are generic and not tailored towards the individual needs of the students, presentation of IEP objectives that do not address all areas of need, and completion of IEP goals that do not promote educational movement forward (Christle & Yell, 2010). While attempting to meet all of the requirements within IDEA, the school-based team may lose its focus on the true intent of IDEA, which is to guarantee the provision of FAPE to students regardless of ability.

Grade-Level Standards in Special Education:
The Effects of NCLB

Although the creation of IDEA made public schools more accountable for the success of students with disabilities, the addition of NCLB has heightened accountability levels to an even higher degree. Locson (2009) reviewed the ways this accountability can be encouraged and monitored within special education. In response to the demand for increased output from students with disabilities, schools have been implementing a variety of changes in how staff is educated and how they can maximize the success of their students. Increasingly, the response of schools has been to push educators to strive for higher standardized test scores to show achievement. One way this effort is being made is through the federal requirement that IEPs must be aligned with the objectives based on the state's academic content standards for the child's corresponding grade in order to meet NCLB requirements that students must be educated with grade-level curriculum. There may be variance in academic standards between states, but the mandate of standards-based objectives must be implemented across the board.

In Texas, for example, the Texas Essential Knowledge and Skills (TEKS) dictate the general education curriculum and thus students' IEP objectives. The idea of TEKS-based objectives came from the NCLB requirement to achieve certain outcomes in reading, math, and science, as well as the IDEA requirements that students must demonstrate progression forward in the general curriculum through the creation of objectives that allow demonstrable progress as related to that curriculum. Prior to NCLB and IDEA requirements, although students were guaranteed access to FAPE, there were no specific guidelines to say what FAPE was, or how to implement it.

As noted earlier, every student in special education is guided by an Individual Education Plan, or IEP, with one of the main elements of that plan being the IEP goals/objectives. Students who receive special education services have goals that are supposed to be focused on their current level of function, but that also must be aligned with grade-level objectives. As long as a child is making progress in his or her educational setting, the program in which he or she is placed is judged to be appropriate. Although this was originally designed to ensure progress, it has turned into another regulation that can impede a child's ability to reach his or her full functional potential, regardless of what that may be. Of course, these regulations were put into place because of abuses in the system, but the goal to constantly be moving forward and avoiding an educational plateau does not mean that every regulation should just be tossed out because it has failed some students. Rather, it must be refined to correct these issues and to improve the system, so as to prevent children from falling through the cracks.

The creation of grade-level standards-based IEP objectives has been widely reviewed. Courtade and Browder (2016) outlined a standards-based IEP as "an IEP that incorporates grade level appropriate academic goals based on state standards or alternate achievement standards" (p. 10). Courtade and Browder further explained how to achieve alignment through creation of goals that ideally address grade-level standards while addressing the functional level of each student. Their outline for the reasoning behind the alignment was threefold:

1. Aligning IEPs with state standards would help prepare students prepare for state assessments (tying into the NCLB requirements).
2. Alignment would also allow students to receive appropriate academic instruction in order to make demonstrable academic progress (tying into IDEA requirements).
3. Having well-aligned IEP goals would give teachers the ability to provide meaningful academic instruction and prioritize educational goals. (pp. 12–13)

Courtade and Browder are very clear in their stance that for a child with a disability, the goal should remain to maximize the overall functional and academic ability of that child. However, when theory is turned into practice, the individuality factor always ends up shining a light on shortcomings. While the concept is noble, the requirement of state standards-based objectives for students receiving special education services is negatively affecting the education of many students under the special education umbrella. Outcomes for students educated in the special education system suggest that the system is failing (e.g., Morgan, Frisco, Farkas, & Hibel, 2010). As the following cases show, overestimating or underestimating a child's ability and potential leads to inappropriate IEP objectives, despite their alignment with state standards. One of these cases will illustrate the outcome when a child is presented with nonfunctional IEP goals far above his cognitive ability with no consideration for the learning of true life skills (which were actually needed and would have been of the greatest benefit). The second of these cases will illustrate the outcome when a child is given goals far below cognitive ability, based solely on physical impairment, limiting her ability to participate at her maximal capability.

CASE STUDIES

Case #1

Jamie, a 14-year-old child with severe autism, was a participator in the life skills program at his middle school in Texas. He had participated in life skills since his entry into public school, but his issue related to grade-level TEKS objectives gradually came to light over the course of his education. Jamie struggled with behavioral issues and limited communicative ability. His mother was the sole caregiver in the home and coordinated home health speech therapy and occupational therapy to help maximize his potential in the home setting. He began receiving both speech and occupational therapy in 2009. His home health goals were focused on increasing functional communication skills and improving his ability to participate in routine tasks in the home setting. During therapy, Jamie would demonstrate behaviors such as jumping up and pushing furniture on top of others, trying to run away, grabbing and pulling hair or other body parts, spitting, and more. Sessions in the home were intense, but Jamie made slow, steady progress with the participation of his mother throughout therapy sessions and largely as result of her willingness to try to implement strategies in the home setting.

During this time, Jamie's mother began to become frustrated with his reported performance and behavior at school. Things that she was working hard to address at home, such as toilet training, brushing teeth, and independent completion of other functional tasks, were not being reinforced at school. Indeed, Jamie was actually regressing while in school. He was constantly trying to run away (a feat that he accomplished while in school several times), he was not encouraged to use the bathroom at school, and he would wet himself throughout the day. The teachers reported to Jamie's mother that he would not do anything they asked or participate in structured tasks, so his mother started to become involved with the daily activities occurring at the school. She began paying attention to his educational goals, which caused her to question their appropriateness. She also requested guidance from the therapists working with him in the home. Upon review, Jamie was found to have goals such as "point to Texas on a map of the United States at 70%" and "identify and match upper and lower letters of the alphabet at 70%." All of his goals did indeed match up to the requirement that goals must be aligned to grade-level TEKS, but none of them were beneficial. He struggled to participate in any structured tasks, much less ones far above his ability level. Anyone working with Jamie knew that all of these objectives were beyond him, but despite teacher reports of being unable to manage behavior at school, progress reports showed that steady progress was being made towards mastery of every single IEP goal each reporting period. The first reporting period, every single goal was reported to be mastered at 15%. The second reporting period, every single goal was reported to be mastered at 25%. The third reporting period, all objectives were reported to be mastered at 40%, the next reporting period all were reported to be at 55%, and of course, the final report showed that all goals were mastered at 70%.

During this time, Jamie's mother requested that he work on functional tasks and behavior so that he could maximize his overall level of independence or at least not regress in his ability to complete functional tasks. However, in the eighth grade, there were no appropriate TEKS-level objectives to meet his functional needs and push him to his maximal capability. The requirement for teachers to address grade-level TEKS with Jamie, who was not toilet-trained and could not care for himself, truly limited him from being able to reach his maximal level of independence. His mother attempted to observe Jamie in class 22 times during this time of contention between her and the school. Despite the progress being reported, she was unable to observe Jamie achieving any of the grade-level goals supposedly being addressed (at reportedly increasing rate of mastery throughout the school year). The school reported that he would complete these goals only when she was not present, but when she was present, they were not even being attempted.

The parent began to advocate for more appropriate goals. She knew that the goals presented were inappropriate and beyond Jamie's ability at that time. However, in her fight for more appropriate goals, she was shut down by the Admission, Review, and Dismissal (ARD) committee, who as a whole stated that Jamie was completing the goals as reported and was making appropriate educational progress, which meant there was no need to modify anything pertaining to his educational placement or goals. They refused to show evidence of his ability to complete any of the goals by videotaping, and his mother was unable to observe him even addressing the goals in any of her 22 documented visits to observe him at the school. As a result of this refusal to address her concerns, she then had to advocate for change by arguing that Jamie was in fact not progressing as reported, and therefore was not receiving an appropriate education at that time. Through arguments at ARDs, it became increasingly evident that the teachers were drowning. They were unable to describe how they addressed various goals, and they also brought up the other children that they were working with, describing the difficulty of managing the various abilities in the classroom. The teacher working with Jamie was unable to define what mastery at 70% even meant. In order to keep their jobs, the teachers needed to write goals aligned with grade-level TEKS, try to address these goals, and then make sure Jamie made adequate progress towards mastery of these objectives, even though his true ability actually prevented it.

This case is an extreme yet illustrative example of how the requirement for grade-level standards in IEPs can limit not only a student's ability to reach his or her maximal level of educational attainment, but also the student's possibility of becoming a functional member of society. If over the course of his entire public school education Jamie had worked on toilet training, food preparation, self-care, and ability to participate in structured, functional tasks, would he be in a different place? Perhaps. What is certain is that failure to even address functional skills and misrepresentation of Jamie's actual academic attainment precluded his ability to achieve meaningful educational progress.

There is another extreme to the failures caused by the requirement of TEKS-based objectives. In the previously discussed case, Jamie was pushed to complete tasks that were not only inappropriate for a child in life skills to be addressing, but also far above his ability level. However, in other situations, the opposite occurs. In these situations, children are limited by their goals, which are far below their ability level but still meet the requirement of alignment to grade-level standards. Children who are under the special education umbrella are only expected to master their IEP goals with grade level standards to demonstrate they are making adequate progress in their educational environment, even when those goals are well below ability level.

Case #2

At the age of three, Mikah was placed in a Preschool Program for Children with Disabilities (PPCD), which is a special education program within the public school setting. Her primary diagnosis was spina bifida, which led to her placement in PPCD under an Other Health Impairment label, but she also had a severe articulation impairment characterized by the presence of phonological processes (or sound errors). However, despite her reduced intelligibility, she was able to score in the above average range on language assessments. She had no cognitive impairments and was very intelligent, with a keen social sense.

From the start of her PPCD placement, Mikah was given extremely simple IEP goals that were geared not towards her academic capability but instead to her physical limitations. Her goals were focused on simple participatory skills such as maintaining attention within a group. She received speech therapy on a consultative basis within the school, and none of her speech therapy goals focused on age-appropriate sound acquisition or suppression of phonological processes, despite her severe articulation delay.

At the start of her kindergarten year, Mikah began speech therapy in the home setting, as her mother felt her progress in school was limited. A speech assessment was completed, and Mikah was again diagnosed with a severe articulation delay with presence of phonological processes. Language abilities were above average despite difficulties with intelligibility. Speech therapy in the home setting was provided twice a week (45 minutes sessions) with goals to address correction of sounds in error, elimination of phonological processes, as well as improving phonemic awareness to aid in reading (as Mikah was in her kindergarten year). In her therapy sessions, Mikah made excellent progress, demonstrated a passion for learning, and displayed excitement with each objective that she was able to master.

Unfortunately, her experience in the public school system was far different. Teachers were complaining that during her time of integration in the mainstream kindergarten class (where she spent a small portion of her day), she didn't participate well and couldn't complete the work the other children were doing. However, her IEP goals within the PPCD classroom (essentially a self-contained life skills classroom, where she spent the rest of her time) were not academic in the least and included objectives such as being able to button pants and participate in circle time. This revelation was shocking, given her strong performance in the home setting.

Mikah began to work on reading related to phonological awareness during her speech therapy sessions and participated in additional reading activities after therapy sessions in the home were completed. Within two to three months, she was able to read multiple sight words and sound out simple consonant-vowel-consonant words. She enjoyed reading and took pride in her success. Despite this progress, instead of moving her towards a general education program with accommodations for her physical impairments, the school pushed to keep her in the special education setting to meet her needs, with continued presentation of inappropriate goals. Not only were they suggesting she remain in special education, but they wanted to place her in a life skills setting as opposed to an inclusion setting that would put her in general education for most of her school time. The school reportedly went so far as to tell Mikah's mother that they would not have an aide to be with her and change her colostomy bag if she participated in general education, and also told her mother that other children would probably make fun of her because of the colostomy bag.

This entire scenario belies what inclusion was originally supposed to be about. Special education was originally designed after story upon story of children who were cognitively able to participate in education being denied due to physical impairments such as blindness or deafness, among other things. This situation, in which the school was denying access to appropriate education by using a medical diagnosis, is the very reason that IDEA was created and that grade-level standards-based IEPs were required: to keep children with special needs from falling through the cracks through lack of equal access to age-appropriate curriculum.

In the end, by limiting Mikah's academic movement forward, the school was actually increasing her frustration and hatred of even being there. She started to act out and refused to participate. Because she was socially keen, she knew the teachers didn't really want to work with her, so she decided she didn't really want to work with them. Mikah had the intellectual capability to excel in the general educational setting, giving her the opportunity to pursue the career of her choice. But if left in the special education setting, she would continue on the path of frustration, moving further and further from typical academic development. Even if she continued in this situation for a few years, the damage would be irreversible. She would be so academically behind that she would never be able to catch up.

As this situation continued, she succumbed to program expectations. The school system had decided that she couldn't do anything, but the reality was she had just stopped trying. Between this and the school's convincing argument to the mother that Mikah would be emotionally traumatized if she had to participate in the general education setting with her physical limitations (which at that time was only the colostomy bag), Mikah continued in the special education system with limited time in general education.

At first glance, these cases seem totally different, and on an individual level, they are. The school system gave Mikah goals that were too simple, and did not allow her to learn at her max capability. The school pushed to keep in her special education due to her physical disability and gave her goals that pulled her away from progressing with her age-level peers. If she continued down that path, she would most likely end up with a large academic gap (due to lack of instruction), which would prevent her from successfully re-entering general education in only a few years' time. This case demonstrates how goals, while meeting the grade-level standards requirement, could actually limit a student's progression forward at his or her true ability level.

In contrast, the school system gave Jamie goals that were too difficult and not functional. Teachers reported progress that was not actually being made and kept increasing the difficulty of the goals to ensure that Jamie was demonstrating progress in his academic setting (even though this "progress" was continually falsified to meet this standard). In trying to address these goals, if they were even attempted, Jamie regressed behaviorally. Jamie would have benefited from a program aimed at increasing independence in activities of daily living, and decreasing the restrictiveness of his environment. Again, although to a different extreme, this case demonstrates how goals, while meeting the grade-level standards requirement, could actually limit a student's progression.

DISCUSSION AND RECOMMENDATIONS

Mismatch between IEP Goals and Students' Ability and Potential

These cases demonstrate problems that have existed since the creation of special education, especially the case of Mikah, where children with disabilities are not pushed to their maximal ability. The idea of grade-level IEP objectives was designed to avoid these situations, so why aren't these regulations able to prevent the problems that occurred within the two cases presented? IEP goals are supposed to be individualized and based on the strengths and weaknesses of each student, while maintaining alignment to state standards-based objectives. However, in Mikah's case, while her weaknesses related to her physical condition were readily addressed, her academic progress was minimized because her program success was only defined by mastery of her overly-simple IEPs, without any effort to even assess or address her strengths. If a child doesn't have any other issues that would prevent normal academic movement forward, there is no excuse for this. Because there are insufficient checks and balances within the current system, it is common for children who are intellectually capable of completing grade-level curriculum to instead make minimal academic movement forward. There are parallels in Jamie's case as well. By initially creating goals based on strengths and weaknesses, then requiring him to demonstrate constant movement forward on standards-based objectives far beyond his ability level, his educational plan became unobtainable and was definitely not individualized.

A second failure within this system is that children are participating in a program that allows them to demonstrate progress only as measured by mastery of IEP goals. Usually, these measures of a student's progress are the primary means of determining the appropriateness of their educational placement. However, this presents two major issues: goals may be simplified to ensure progress without promoting maximal capability (as we see in Mikah's case), or goals may be too complex for a student with severe disabilities because they must be aligned with grade-level standards in all subject areas, which may cause teachers to report progress that isn't actually being made (as we see in Jamie's case). Again, despite the extreme individual differences, the root of the problem is the same.

IEP Reform

It is time to continue the refinement of the special education system by solving this root problem in an effort to improve outcomes in special education as a whole. The public educational system is for everyone, and until everyone has the same ability to achieve maximal success, reforms must be made. One possibility is to formulate an educational program based on the best educational setting. This idea has been seen in creation of life skills, structured learning, and resource/inclusion settings, but regardless of setting, the standards-based objectives still rule supreme. If progress were measured with more flexibility as well as being setting dependent, there could be more appropriate individualized educational plans across all settings. For example, life skills IEP requirements could be based on the SMART method, a concept introduced by Jung (2007). Jung viewed IEP goals as the foundation of a child's education plan, but just as important as *what* goals were to be implemented was *how* they were to be implemented. The SMART acronym stands for specific, measurable, attainable, routine-based, and tied to a functional priority. Another acronym Jung (2007) uses is ROUTINE, which stands for routines based, outcome-related, understandable, transdisciplinary, implemented by family AND teacher, nonjudgmental, and evidence-based.

Some of these ideas are already in place in school systems, such as making measurable goals. But other ideas presented are not used enough, such as making goals trans-disciplinary, routine-based, and tied to a functional priority. While a goal such as "point to Texas on a map with 70% accuracy" is specific and measurable, it is not routine based, nor is it tied to a functional priority, and it may not even be attainable (as it was not in Jamie's case). When this strategy is applied, all staff working with the child must be aware of a target goal, as well as how to implement that goal across activities that will be completed during the day. This type of approach would be much more beneficial for a student like Jamie, although it may be only minimally necessary for a student participating in a more inclusion-based setting.

For children in the resource or inclusion setting, progress should be measured by academic movement forward. This could be achieved by obtaining a grade-level baseline and then assessing movement forward through quarterly assessments. A child might not complete a grade each year, but over the course of his or her participation in the public school setting, the goal would be to slowly master each grade at the student's maximal rate possible. The idea of using evaluation to assess movement and aid in forming appropriate objectives has been suggested as a tool to use across special education settings (Youtsey, 2003). A child might graduate with a mastery of sixth grade curriculum, but that mastery would make employment possible.

It is, of course, essential that students be exposed to grade-level curriculum, that teachers have high expectations for students, and that even students with severe disabilities receive meaningful academic instruction. However, when a constant push for grade-level standards is required, to the exclusion of functional goals and without teachers actually knowing how to address and measure the standards-based objectives, students end up getting lost in the process. They may end up walking across a stage at graduation without possessing the ability to read, or worse still, end up not even walking across the stage in the first place.

To address this issue, we must consider the variety of social justice themes relevant to special education. While new proposals can always be presented to try to regulate the formation of appropriate education plans, staff integrity must be improved across the board. The problems that have been discussed related to implementation of IDEA (e.g., McLaughlin, 2010) also largely result from poor administration, lazy application of IEPs, and lack of intervention from the many available resources within every public school setting. In Mikah's case, teachers decided that she should only address her IEP goals with no effort to push her forward during her general education time (going so far as to tell the parent she couldn't do any regular education work despite evidence indicating otherwise).

In Jamie's case, teachers and therapists blatantly falsified progress reports. These problems are further exacerbated by lack of teacher understanding of how to create and implement specially designed instruction. Jamie's teacher didn't even know what 70% mastery meant, much less what a more appropriate path would be for him. So while pushing to change regulations might be a start, it is the totality of change that must occur for true reform to take place. While we now accept disability of part of the human experience, we still have to work to remedy the inequalities that continue to exist in the treatment of individuals with disabilities and strive to produce outcomes that parallel what we see for those without disabilities.

REFERENCES

Christle, C. A., & Yell, M. L. (2010). Individualized education programs: Legal requirements and research findings. *Exceptionality, 18*(3), 109–123.

Conner, D. (2014). Social justice in education for students with disabilities. In L. Florian (Ed.), *The SAGE handbook of special education* (2nd ed., pp. 111–128). Los Angeles: SAGE.

Courtrade, G., & Browder, D. (2016). *Aligning IEPs to the Common Core State Standards for students with moderate and severe disabilities.* Verona, WI: Attainment Company.

Education for All Handicapped Children Act of 1975, Pub. L. No. 94–142, 89 Stat. 773 (1975).

Etscheidt, S., & Curran, C.M. (2010). Peer-reviewed research and individualized education programs (IEPs): An examination of intent and impact. *Exceptionality, 18*(3), 138–150.

IDEA Improvement Act of 1997, Pub. L. No. 105-17, 111 Stat. 37 (1997).

Individuals with Disabilities Education Act of 1990, Pub. L. No. 101–476, 104 Stat. 1103 (1990).

Individuals with Disabilities Education Improvement Act of 2004, Pub. L. No. 108-446, 118 Stat. 2647 (2004).

Jung, L. A. (2007). Writing SMART objectives and strategies that fit the ROUTINE. *Teaching Exceptional Children, 39*(4), 54–58.

Locson, L. (2009). Accountability-driven school reform model for special education: A Delphi study. (Unpublished doctoral dissertation). University of Texas, Austin: TX.

Martin, E., Martin R., & Terman, D. (1996). The legislative and litigation history of special education. *The Future of Children, 6*(1), 25–39.

McLaughlin, M. J. (2010). Evolving interpretations of educational equity and students with disabilities. *Exceptional Children, 76*(3), 265–278.

Morgan, P. L., Frisco, M., Farkas, G., & Hibel, J. (2010). A propensity score matching analysis of the effects of special education services. *Journal of Special Education, 43(4)*, 236-254.

No Child Left Behind Act of 2001, Pub. L. No. 107-110, 115 Stat. 1425 (2001).

Weishaar, P. M. (2010). Twelve ways to incorporate strengths-based planning into the IEP process. *The Clearing House, 83*, 207–210.

Yell, M. L., Katsiyannis, A., Losinski, M., & Marshall, K. (2016). Peer-reviewed research and the IEP: Implications of Ridley School District v. M.R. and J.R. ex rel. E.R. (2012). *Intervention in School and Clinic, 51(4)*, 253-257.

Youtsey, D. (2003). Standards reform in special education. *Leadership, 32*(3), 22-25

Chapter 7

WHAT IS SPECIALLY DESIGNED INSTRUCTION?

AMY TEN NAPEL

INTRODUCTION

Special education. What is it and what is it supposed to be? Federal law indicates that special education is specially designed instruction. In working with teachers and providing consultation in both special education and general education settings, it is alarming to discover the number of professional educators who have never heard the term specially designed instruction (SDI), much less the description of it provided in the regulations associated with Individuals with Disabilities Education Improvement Act of 2004.

Why is this important? A publication from The National Center for Educational outcomes concludes that for students with disabilities, "the vast majority (80-85 percent) can meet the same standards as other students if they are given the specially designed instruction, appropriate access, supports, and accommodations, as required by IDEA" (Thurlow, Quenemoen, & Lazarus, 2011, p. 4). Furthermore, Thurlow and colleagues state that there should only be a small percentage of students with disabilities who may require alternate achievement standards, and those students, when given high-quality instruction in grade-level curriculum, can achieve more than they have in the past.

Students with disabilities can learn. When they are not learning or progressing as expected, some would believe that the cause is within the child and expectations are lowered. Instead, Donnellan has said that "we should assume that poor performance is due to instructional inadequacy rather than to student deficits" (as cited in Jorgensen, 2005, para. 3). We should never blame the child; rather, we should always be looking for ways to accelerate learning by providing intensive and strategic instruction. We expect progress from all students, and it is mandated by federal law for students with disabilities. However, Hettleman (2013) observes that

> . . . in general, school systems across the country apply a low, minimalist standard for how much progress students with disabilities should be enabled and expected to achieve under IDEA and other federal laws. This standard is typically expressed in terms of "some benefit" that is "meaningful." (p. 6)

Hettleman asserts that some school systems embrace these vague terms in an attempt to minimize the responsibility of the educator. Ultimately, this results in lowered expectations of student progress.

BACKGROUND

While trends in the data suggest that students with disabilities are making progress, statistics continue to show discrepancies in test performance between students with disabilities and their peers without disabilities. Students identified with disabilities often have scores 30–40 percentage points lower in reading and in math, compared to their peers without disabilities (Center on Education Policy, 2009). These differences are not just a special education problem. It is a problem that includes general educators as well. The majority of students with disabilities are receiving at least some of their instruction in a general education environment. Data from the National Center for Education Statistics (Snyder, de Brey, & Dillow, 2016) for students ages 6–21 during the school year 2013–14 indicate the following in regards to educational environment:

- 62% spent most of the school day (i.e., 80% or more of time) in general classes.
- 19% spent 40 to 79% of the school day in general classes.
- 14% spent less than 40% of time inside general classes (Snyder et al., 2016, Table 204.60).

With the large numbers of students with disabilities spending the majority of their instructional day in general education settings, the need for understanding and implementation of specially designed instruction is relevant to all.

The provision of specially designed instruction may mean that something is "different" for a student with a disability. Different typically leads to the issue of fairness. Is fair to do the same thing for each student the same way with no exception? Or is fair to provide what each student needs? Wormeli (2006) opines that fairness is appropriateness, not one-size-fits-all. U.S. law requires public schools to provide a free appropriate public education (FAPE) for students with disabilities (34 C.F.R. §300.17). In the current discussion, the term fair will represent those things that students require as a result of their disability.

A common theme related to social justice in education is the inequity in opportunities and outcomes for minority groups (Blum, Wilson, & Patish, 2015). As mentioned above, most students with disabilities can learn when provided specially designed instruction. The fact that their outcomes are continually and consistently discrepant from their peers without disabilities should be alarming. Rather than simply stating that a problem exists, more attention and emphasis should be placed on how to fix it. How can these discrepancies be addressed under the current systems in place in the United States? One way is to consider what the law says special education is. Using the definition provided in federal law, breaking down and defining each component, and thoughtfully applying the concepts to each student with a disability are essential for developing an appropriate and fair education program.

Federal education regulations state in 34 CFR § 300.39 (a)(1), "Special education means specially designed instruction, at no cost to the parents, to meet the unique needs of a child with a disability." The regulations go on to define the term in 34 CFR § 300.39 (b)(3) in the following manner:

(3) Specially designed instruction means adapting, as appropriate to the needs of an eligible child under this part, the content, methodology, or delivery of instruction--
    (i)   To address the unique needs of the child that result from the child's disability; and

(ii)   To ensure the access of the child to the general curriculum, so that the child can meet the educational standards within the jurisdiction of the public agency that apply to all children.

If, at the very least, these words are taken at face value, there are several things that must be individually considered for each student:

- Unique needs of the child (the disability condition(s) and needs related to the disability)
- General education curriculum (enrolled grade level curriculum)
- Adaptations (accommodations vs modifications)
- Content
- Methodology
- Delivery of Instruction

Other special education regulations require that an individual education program (IEP) be developed for each student each year. The result is a document that should outline all of the supports and services the child must have in order to receive FAPE. Among the hundreds of IEPs we have seen (and written) over the course of our careers, very few could be described as a logical, well thought out, clearly written and understood blue print for the education of the child with a disability. Most IEPs are a convoluted mess, full of statements and check boxes that ensure that all of the federal regulations and any additional state regulations have been considered. These documents are typically designed to reflect compliance rather than a truly individualized program for the student with a disability. Many teachers say that IEP documents are not meaningful and tend to all look alike. Parents may say that the document is not user-friendly and is difficult to read and comprehend.

In order to help consumers of the IEP (e.g., special education teachers, general education teachers, and parents) better understand what special education is and/or should be, the components of SDI must be further examined. The terminology provided in federal law is not specifically defined in the regulations. Operational definitions of the terms are provided to lay a foundational groundwork on which the framework for the application of SDI can be based.

Unique Needs

When considering the unique needs of a student with a disability, a thorough evaluation of the student must first be conducted. The information in the evaluation becomes the basis for the IEP that is eventually developed. The evaluation should be comprehensive in nature and consider all areas of suspected disability. Not only must the evaluation identify whether a disability condition is present, it must also include information related to enabling the student to be involved in and make progress in the general education curriculum (34 CFR § 300.304).

The evaluation process requires more than just identifying that a disability is present. Oftentimes that information is not a surprise to anyone involved with the student's education. A referral would not have been initiated if difficulties were not already observed and documented. It is the federal requirement to include information that enables the student to be involved in and make progress in the general curriculum that might be lacking sufficient detail. This information is imperative in order to draft an appropriate IEP that outlines supports and services necessary for the student as a result of the disability.

General Education Curriculum

Curriculum standards are defined by each state. Whatever general education curriculum is used, all members of the IEP team should have knowledge about what it entails, though certainly there will be varying levels of expertise. The idea, however, is that the team members should have enough information about the curricular expectations for general education students to have a conversation about where the student with a disability will encounter barriers in the curriculum. The program that is ultimately developed is designed to provide the student with a disability access to the general education in spite of the disability. While an IEP can identify skill deficits and implement interventions to try and remediate them, the purpose of the IEP is to provide the student access to, so he or she can make progress in, the general education curriculum.

Adaptations

There is a misconception that the purpose of special education is to provide a program for students with disabilities that is lower, slower, and/or different from the general education curriculum. Federal law does not define the word adaptation, but for purposes of this discussion, adaptation will be considered accommodations or modifications. These terms are not synonymous. There are important distinctions between these terms.

Accommodations are those things that change the "how" of learning. They "are intended to reduce or even eliminate the effects of a student's disability but do not reduce the learning expectations" (Texas Education Agency, 2015, p. 6). Once appropriate accommodations that meet the unique needs of the learner related to the disability are made, students with disabilities can meet the standards set forth for all students (Twachtman-Cullen & Twachtman-Bassett, 2011). Accommodations help students access both content and instruction and allow the student to accurately demonstrate what he or she knows (Nolet & McLaughlin, 2005).

Modifications change the "what" of learning (Texas Education Agency, 2015). The nature of the task or target skill as defined in the standard or curriculum is altered and performance expectations are changed. Modifications are not simply teaching students at a lower grade level. They are changes that are thoughtfully planned and tightly aligned to enrolled grade-level standards (Iris Center for Training Enhancement, 2004). Modifications should be implemented only after all accommodations have been exhausted, as they result in the student not having access to the full breadth and depth of the mandated curriculum.

It is important to note that the only way to know whether something is an accommodation or modification is to reference the original standard in the general education curriculum. A determination must be made as to what the strategy that is being implemented actually does to the standard. If it offsets the impact of the disability without changing the content standard or performance expectation, it is an accommodation. If it changes or alters the content standard or performance expectation, it is a modification (Iris Center for Training Enhancement, 2004). The exact same strategy in one situation may be an accommodation but in another situation could be a modification. It all depends on the intent of the standard.

Content

Content can be defined as the state standards. Content includes both the breadth and depth of what students are expected to learn for the grade level in which the student is enrolled. The Office of Special Education and Rehabilitative Services (OSERS) issued a Dear Colleagues letter in November 2015 to address the meaning or intent of the term general education curriculum. The letter states that the general education curriculum is "the same curriculum as for nondisabled children" (U.S. Department of Education, 2015, p. 2) and that the IEP must be aligned with the state's academic content standards for the grade in which the child is enrolled.

Methodology and Delivery of Instruction

Methodology refers to evidence-based practice. These are best practices in the field of education that have been shown to be effective by peer-reviewed research. Delivery of instruction can be thought of as the implementation of the evidence-based practice or methodology. This is the explicit explanation of how the methodology will be applied. It is the nuts and bolts of the instructional design or what specialized instruction for a particular child should look like.

THREE-STEP FRAMEWORK FOR SPECIALIZED INSTRUCTION

With a better understanding of the components of specially designed instruction, a three-step framework (Region 4 Education Service Center, 2016) for application of the concept can help IEP teams to plan more appropriate and descriptive programs and help improve outcomes for students with disabilities.

- Step 1: Determine how the student's disability impacts his or her access and progress in the enrolled grade level curriculum.
- Step 2: Determine what specially designed instruction is needed for the student to access and make progress in the enrolled grade-level curriculum.
- Step 3: Describe the adaptations needed based upon the specific needs resulting from the disability.

Step 1

In the first step, the IEP team must have a complete understanding of the student's disability and the unique needs arising from it. This information is first documented in the student's special education evaluation and further described in the present levels of academic achievement and functional performance that is a required component of the IEP. "Without adequate knowledge of both the disability itself and the way in which it affects a particular student, it is impossible to determine the strategies, supports, or conditions that are helpful to the student" (Twachtman-Cullen & Twachtman-Bassett, 2011, p. 25).

Step 2

The second step is to specifically consider what specially designed instruction is needed, that is, how the content, methodology, and delivery of instruction will be adapted based on the unique needs of the student. Each component should be individually and thoroughly considered.

Content

Feifer and De Fina (2000) have noted, "Many special education classes in our schools are curricular-driven (sic), which is nothing more than slower-paced instruction, as opposed to a specially designed strategic intervention plan targeted to enhance the student's unique learning ability" (p. 7). To guard against this, all the decisions regarding the adaptation of content should be made through the lens of the enrolled grade-level curriculum. Students must have access to and afforded the opportunity to make progress in the same curriculum and content as their peers in spite of their disability. No matter what the disability or level at which the student can independently function, access to the general education curriculum should always be a priority. This might be through accommodations, modifications, or for students with the most significant cognitive disabilities requiring alternate achievement standards, through prerequisite skills.

The real issue when considering access to the curriculum becomes how we can help the student compensate in spite of the disability. Compensation can be defined as procedures, techniques, and strategies that are intended to bypass or minimize the impact of the disability (Mascolo, Alfonso, & Flanagan, 2014). Too often, the focus is on the student's functional level and what he or she can do independently, rather than what the student can do with supports. Sometimes educators and parents believe, with good intentions, that basic skills must be addressed and mastered before students can have access to higher-level concepts and skills. McLaughlin (2005) has pointed out that it is problematic to wait until students have mastered basic skills before tackling challenging standards, as doing so will often result in students never having the opportunity to work on these challenging standards. This is not to say that remediation is not an important consideration, but it should be in addition to, and not to the exclusion of, the enrolled grade-level curriculum. Focusing efforts on remediation, especially for older students, creates a larger gap between where the student is and where the student should be.

Accessing content through accommodations should be the first consideration, as this does not change the nature of the task or target skill. The learning expectations are the same as those of students without disabilities. One way to think of it is that all students cross the same finish line, even though the student with a disability might take a different route to get there. Applying the principles of universal design for learning (UDL) by providing multiple means of representation, expression, and engagement (Center for Applied Special Technology, 2011) is an evidenced-based practice that can help educators understand that doing something different for a student doesn't automatically mean that content has been modified.

Accessing content through modifications means that breadth of the curriculum, the depth or complexity of the curriculum, or both has been changed. This should be a decision that is very thoughtfully considered, because once this occurs, the student will not likely be prepared for the next grade level, which can lead to larger gaps. If the IEP actually determines modified content is required for a student with a disability, the discussion and documentation should include whether the breadth, depth, or both will be altered. If the breadth is altered, standards for which the student will not be responsible for learning should be identified. If depth is altered, the complexity of the content will have to be considered and the level at which the student can be expected to achieve identified. It may be necessary to alter both the breadth and depth due to the impact of the disability.

Accessing content through prerequisite skills may be required for some students with significant cognitive disabilities. Nonetheless, these students still require access to their enrolled grade-level curriculum. For this population, some educators and parents may feel that learning functional skills, such as self-care, is more of a priority than academic skills. It is important to discuss with those who hold this position that access to the general education is a federal requirement and the right of a student with a disability. Although functional skills may be incorporated into and reinforced during lessons, having access to and making progress in the curriculum should be the primary focus. Students can learn the concepts and big ideas of content areas that other students their age are learning, even if it is at a significantly lower level. For example, when concepts of biology are addressed in the general education curriculum, students accessing through prerequisite skills can be learning about living and nonliving things, plants, animals, etc., using academic language. Similarly, students may learn about solids and liquids in chemistry. A cooking activity may be presented later, which provides an additional context in which to reinforce the chemistry vocabulary and concepts as applied to a functional skill. This is quite different from simply teaching cooking without any academic context.

Remediation can also be considered, but again, it should not be provided in the place of the enrolled grade-level curriculum. Remediation can be defined as techniques or programs used to ameliorate cognitive and academic deficits. Academic interventions typically focus on developing skills, increasing the automaticity of skills, or improving the application of skills (Mascolo et al., 2014). If particular skills are identified for remediation, the ensuing discussion should address the following questions.

- **Has the skill been explicitly taught?**

This is an important question. There can be many reasons that a student has gaps in learning. Schools and school districts do not always follow the same scope and sequence of the state-mandated curriculum, so students who move or change schools may miss out on pertinent instruction. Absences of the student or perhaps absences of the teacher could also contribute to learning gaps. Sometimes students are in the same school with good attendance and have missed important instruction because they were accessing the curriculum through modifications or were receiving supports and services in a more restrictive environment that impacted their access to the enrolled grade-level curriculum.

- **Is it necessary to teach the skill given the age, grade, and developmental level of the student?**

This particular question can be shocking to some. The question does not imply that instruction in basic skills and remediation is unimportant. The intent of the question is more about appropriateness. For example, there may be a student who was identified as having a learning disability that impacts basic reading skills in elementary school. Much time has been spent over the years on instruction and remediation in this area. At some point, perhaps in junior high or high school, the IEP team should examine whether or not to continue providing explicit instruction in this area and instead focus on how the student can better access the curriculum in spite of the difficulty in basic reading skills. This could include teaching the student to use technology, such as a text to speech program, so that content can be accessed through other means besides the student reading it independently.

- **Is there a current plan in place to remediate skills?**

If so, what is it? The plan must identify what specially designed instruction is being provided and how much progress has been made. A decision should be made to continue the current plan, revise it, or to develop a new plan.

- **What are the specifics of the plan?**

There must be an understanding of all the stakeholders as to the roles and responsibilities of school staff, the student, and even the parents. This includes who will provide the instruction, what will be taught, along with where, when, and how it will be taught. There should be some accountability and review built in as well to ensure the quality of instruction, participation of the student, and any supports provided by the parents, as the amount of progress will likely be impacted if the plan is not followed. If the IEP team has decided that remediation is necessary, it is too important to leave these things to chance.

- **How will the student continue to have access to the enrolled grade-level curriculum?**

Again, the remediation is in addition to, not the replacement of, the enrolled grade-level curriculum. These content-related concepts are illustrated in Figure 7.1.

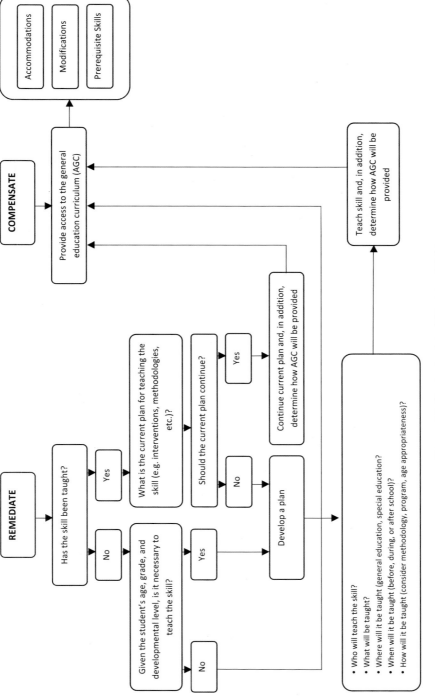

Figure 7.1 Content-related Decision Making.

Methodology

Best teaching practices are based upon evidence. Continual learning and study are necessary for educational professionals to stay abreast of current research. There is concern, however, that teacher preparation programs and continuing professional development in this area are lacking. Hettleman (2013) cites the lack of educator knowledge of evidence-based best practices for the identification and treatment of disabilities, especially in the area of reading, as a major contributor to special education students not meeting state academic standards. He further writes that "while there is no exact proof of best instructional practices, a lot more is known about them than is applied in special education" (p. 12). As educators, we must make continuous learning and improvement a priority in order to provide the most effective methodologies to improve student performance and to adhere to the federal mandate that special education services should be "based on peer-reviewed research to the extent practicable" (34 CFR § 300.320 (a)(4)).

Delivery of Instruction

Students with disabilities need explicit instruction (Archer & Hughes, 2011). Those responsible for instructing students with disabilities need explicit guidance as well. Students with disabilities will certainly have access to qualified special education teachers; they will also likely have interaction with and instruction from some who do not have an extensive background in working with students with disabilities. Outlining the delivery of instruction so that all involved know what to do, as well as how to do it and when to do it, will lead to better outcomes for students.

Too often the adaptations that a student needs as a result of his or her disability are not adequately described; such adaptations are often indicated in the form of a box that is checked on a page in the IEP document that indicates an overly generic strategy. The idea is to give the end-user information about application of the strategy. What does the strategy "look like" in practice? For example, scaffolding, chunking information, and checking for understanding are strategies that may be indicated in an IEP. While educational professionals may understand these concepts to some degree, a teacher needs to know how to implement the strategy based on the individual student's needs. Another distinction that may not be considered an actual instructional strategy in an IEP, but provides information regarding needs of the student, is preferential seating. This could mean placement front and center in the classroom near the point of instruction, but it could also mean off to the side to reduce distractions, or near an exit if the student must leave the classroom regularly so as not to call attention to the situation and/ or allow for easier transitions.

Step 3

The third step is a thorough description of the adaptations to content, methodology, and delivery of instruction considered in Step 2. The place where this is supposed to be outlined is in the IEP document. As noted earlier, the IEP document is not always easily understood. In order to formulate an IEP effectively and in enough detail that another teacher could implement the program as intended without any additional information, it may be necessary to deviate from the computerized programs or the compliance driven forms that are commonly used in developing IEPs.

The cases below illustrate the application of this three-step framework to three students with varying educational needs. Each case provides a step-by-step conceptualization and recommendations for how to manage issues of content, methodology, and delivery of specialized instruction.

CASE STUDIES

Case #1

Aaron was a high school student with a learning disability. His IEP indicated that he received inclusion support. Often, this is the totality of the description of services that is documented in the IEP. What is inclusion support, anyway? The operational definition of this term varies from campus to campus and from district to district. Rather than naming the service to be provided, the IEP must describe what the person providing the service should do on behalf of the student prior to the classroom instruction or what should occur in the classroom.

Many times, master scheduling and staff availability, rather than student need, seem to drive the amount of support recommended or provided. Often, general education master schedules are set first and necessary special education supports are an afterthought. Trying to "fit" supports around an already established schedule can result in decisions being made for administrative convenience rather than student need. For example, there are four sections of Biology going on during the same class period, each with students receiving special education services. If there is only one special education teacher available during that period, what are the options?

Let's assume that all of the special education students are placed in one class and that the "inclusion support" is provided every day for the entire class period by a certified special education teacher. Advantages of this option include having two highly qualified teachers in the class together. This could essentially be a considered a "co-teach" setting and could be very beneficial to all of the students in the class if the teachers worked together, planned together, and took shared responsibility for the outcomes of the students. A drawback of this option would be too many students with disabilities in one class. At what point does the class go from a general education setting to a special education setting? If there are too many needs in one class, the rigor of instruction could be compromised, which affects all of the students.

What if the option chosen is to leave all of the students in their various classes and the special education teacher supports all of them? If the class period is 55 minutes, the teacher would provide less than 15 minutes of support per day, or provide a longer duration on alternating days. While this is a possible solution, the implementation can only be successful with meticulous planning and cooperation of all of the teaching staff.

The two options presented above are both typical solutions to the service delivery conundrum. Where in this process were the individual needs of the students considered? If this question cannot be answered, the process is backwards. The availability of resources is a real issue that can impact service provision; however, decisions must still be made based on student need rather than on administrative convenience.

Now we can examine the three steps of specially designed instruction for Aaron, who received his instruction in a general education classroom with supports.

Step 1

Aaron is a student with a learning disability that impacts reading comprehension. Evaluation data indicates that he specifically has difficulty in the areas of lexical knowledge and working memory. When considering the area of lexical knowledge, this means that he has difficulty understanding and using correct vocabulary. The impact of this is that when he is required to access grade-level content, his comprehension of the content is hindered by the academic and/or the content vocabulary present in the reading selection. Aaron's unique needs related to his disability require vocabulary supports.

Aaron also has difficulties with working memory. Dehn (2008) defines working memory as "the management, manipulation, and transformation of information drawn from either short-term or long-term memory . . . whose primary function is to facilitate and enhance the capacity of encoding, storage, and retrieval functions that are essential for learning and higher level processing of information" (p. 58). He describes text comprehension as involving many skills, such as decoding words, lexical knowledge, integration of information from other sentences and paragraphs, determining main idea, etc. Because of deficits in this area, Aaron has difficulty independently reading and comprehending grade-level text, especially those that are lengthy and require higher-ordered thinking.

Step 2

Considerations at this step include the concepts of remediation and compensation. Age and grade level are always factors to consider, as are the specific needs of the student related to the disability. Aaron's difficulties stem from deficits in lexical knowledge and working memory. Given that Aaron is a high school student, remediation of a particular skill may not be warranted. The IEP team may determine that supporting his vocabulary acquisition needs are best accomplished by focusing on vocabulary relevant to the courses and units of study in which he is currently enrolled, rather than focusing on a remedial-type vocabulary acquisition program that does not relate to his current course work. In addition, addressing a working memory deficit with an evidence-based intervention may not be achievable within the confines of the school day. Compensation, therefore, would be the focus of Step 2 for Aaron.

Content is the first consideration of specially designed instruction. Aaron is a student who receives all instruction in a general education classroom with a service delivery model that may be known as mainstream, inclusion, or in-class support. While assignments may be adapted or changed for him, he is capable of accessing and achieving the intent of the state-mandated performance standards. With accommodations that support vocabulary knowledge and working memory, he can be expected to attain the breadth and depth of the curriculum.

There are a host of methodologies and evidence-based practices that are successful in the area of vocabulary development. Five methods of teaching vocabulary identified by the National Reading Panel (2000) include explicit instruction, implicit instruction, multimedia methods, capacity methods, and association methods. Evidence-based practices for supporting working memory include chunking or grouping strategies, direct teaching of rehearsal strategies, mnemonics, external supports such as step-by-step procedures, and eliminating irrelevant information (Dehn, 2008). While all of these strategies may be beneficial for Aaron, the IEP team should discuss which strategies have been tried and for how long, and target those that have been successful in his education so far.

Documenting the delivery of instruction is critical, since it is the road map for the service providers to most effectively implement the evidence-based practice(s). Explicit instruction and errorless learning have proven more helpful for Aaron than implicit instruction, as he has not shown the ability to acquire and apply new words through incidental learning. Multimedia methods and association methods have also been helpful for vocabulary acquisition. Preteaching vocabulary using pictures, providing examples within the correct context, and linking the new words to previously learned material are strategies that can be used in the classroom. The special education teacher providing support in the general education classroom can create an account for Aaron on an online program or application and create a word list or email a word list for him to look up words on line using other digital tools. Aaron can access this site outside of the classroom setting, and the preteaching of vocabulary can be done prior to the actual instruction of the concepts. He can access the computer lab before or after school or during lunch. In addition, his parents indicate he has access to technology and the Internet in the home setting and on his cell phone, so the vocabulary instruction and review can be completed as a homework assignment.

When considering the strategies that support Aaron's working memory, he works better when long passages are chunked into smaller sections and extraneous visual clutter is minimized. If accessing the material using technology, various programs are available that will do this with the click of a button. He has an accommodation that allows him the use of the highlighter, but this requires the assistance of the general education or special education teacher to pinpoint the key ideas or concepts to highlight. His comprehension improves when vocabulary supports are embedded within the chunked passage, which can also be done through technology resources.

Step 3

This is the documentation step of the supports and strategies listed in Step 2. Other things to consider when recording this information are what this type of support looks like and what preparation is required. The types of supports described above cannot be accomplished "on the fly" or by "checking in." Successful implementation of Aaron's program within this type of service delivery model requires supports at the master scheduling level all the way down to daily planning with both the general education and special education staff.

Case #2

Jared received academic instruction in a special education setting that is most often referred to as a resource setting. Sometimes the resource setting is regarded as a "lower and slower" type of instructional delivery model that focuses more on a functional level than on access and progress in the enrolled grade-level curriculum. In many cases, it is a classroom that serves multiple grades and subjects at one time.

Jared was a student in elementary school that serves kindergarten through fifth grade students. It is a small school, and staffing allocations indicate that two teachers should be sufficient to serve the number of special education students at the school. Because the school offers a continuum of services, supports are provided in both general and special education settings for all six grade levels. To serve all students effectively, the special education teacher must have planning time with each grade level in addition to the services that must be delivered. Logistically, of course, this is impossible.

One alternative solution can be to group students by functional level. If Jared were a fourth grader who had difficulty in math, he may have been grouped with any combination of students from kindergarten to fifth grade. When this occurs, the teacher would have a very difficult time aligning the instruction to each student's enrolled grade level standards. Often, an all-for-one, one-for-all type strategy is employed for the mental health and survival of the special education teacher. Thus, access and progress in the enrolled grade-level curriculum takes a back seat.

Let's consider the three-step process for Jared to remain engaged in learning and making progress in the general education curriculum.

Step 1

Jared is a student with the disability condition of an Other Health Impairment for seizures. Although he takes medication for his medical condition, the seizures and/or medications cause slow processing speed and memory difficulties. He also fatigues easily during sustained mental tasks.

Step 2

When considering content, Jared, as an elementary school student, may require some remediation of skills. Independently, he performs below peers in his enrolled grade level in all academic subjects. There are gaps in his learning that can be targeted and direct instruction provided in these areas in addition to accessing the same curriculum as his peers without disabilities. A plan should be developed to identify the specific skill that will be addressed, how the skill will be taught, when and where the instruction will take place, and who is responsible for the implementation and progress monitoring. It is essential for all to understand that the remediation will not take the place of Jared's instruction that is aligned to enrolled grade-level standards.

Jared has disability-related learning needs that make it difficult for him to master the breadth and depth of the state-mandated curriculum. Accommodations are provided that allow adequate time for him to process information, aid his memory, and adapt for times he is fatigued. Modifications, or changes to the nature of the task or target skill of the state standards, are also required as a result of his disability. As stated earlier in the chapter, modifications do not mean simply teaching students at a lower grade level. They are changes that are thoughtfully planned and tightly aligned to enrolled grade-level standards (Iris Center for Training Enhancement, 2004).

Due to the impact of Jared's disability, the IEP team could determine that the breadth of the curriculum should be reduced. The team would need to determine which parts of the curriculum would be addressed and the parts of the curriculum for which he would not be responsible for learning. The IEP team could also consider if the complexity of the curriculum would be altered. For example, when a performance expectation within a standard indicates that a student will evaluate or analyze a particular concept, Jared, as a result of his disability, may be expected to recognize or recall some of the main ideas of the concept. Limiting both the breadth and depth of the curriculum may be warranted; however, it will still be within the enrolled grade level curriculum.

Educational methodologies that align to problems with slow processing speed include providing "wait time" to allow the processing of information, emphasizing quality over quantity, providing extra time to complete assignments, and reduction of copying or note-taking tasks. External supports to aid memory have been useful and should be continued.

Tailoring the delivery of instruction for Jared will focus on ways for him to have repeated exposure to content. This will aid both the processing speed and memory difficulties he experiences. Video or audio recordings of content that can be accessed recurrently provide a practical way for Jared to access the information as many times as needed. Providing him with an outline of class notes prior to discussions will help him worry less about writing and focus more on the information being shared. This will help with fatigue concerns, as will limiting the length of the assignment or test he is required to complete. For example, if an enrolled grade level standard is for a student to write an essay of appropriate length, Jared may be required to write one paragraph with a topic sentence, three supporting details, and a closing sentence. This not only modifies the performance expectation of the standard, but reduces the length of the assignment.

External supports provided, such as steps to solve a problem and an interactive notebook where information and observations are recorded, could be utilized during instruction. However, due to the impact of his disability, Jared may require the use of these supports on assessments as well. When decisions like this are made for students with disabilities, it is imperative that the support be required as a result of the disability and thoughtfully applied. A common complaint or response to these types of supports is that it is not "fair" to other students. When adaptations to content, methodology, or delivery of instruction are provided to a student, it should be because it is required for the student with a disability to have access to and make progress in the enrolled grade level curriculum. It would be unfair to the student with a disability to not provide the specially designed instruction he or she needs because the impact of the disability is such that access and progress cannot be achieved without it.

Step 3

Due to the needs Jared has resulting from his disability, much of his academic instruction will be modified and provided by a special education teacher. This does not negate the importance of detailing his needs in such a manner that anyone could read the IEP document, replicate the specially designed instruction, and not lose any time in trying to figure out what Jared needs. Too often when students change schools, whether because the family has moved or the student has advanced to another grade in another school, teachers talk about getting to know the child and taking time to learn what the student needs. Frankly, there is no time for that. The purpose of the IEP is to have that information ready to go so that no time is wasted.

Case #3

Cody required highly specialized supports and services as a result of his disability. Many teachers, administrators, and parents do not see the need for academic instruction for students like Cody. Access and progress in the general education curriculum is nothing but a check box on a form with materials and resources that may be inadequate or inappropriate given the child's age and enrolled grade level. The "what to do" is as difficult as the "how to do it," given the severity of the student's disabilities and the lack of appropriate resources available for this population. Regardless, educators must continue their efforts to provide SDI and ensure an appropriate program for the student to have access to and make progress in the general education curriculum.

Step 1

Cody is a student with multiple disabilities. He has an intellectual disability, an orthopedic impairment, and an Other Health Impairment because of severe, life threatening medical conditions that must be constantly monitored. Cody does not communicate verbally and uses pointing and eye gaze to indicate his wants and preferences. Assistive technology is used in the classroom and home settings to aid communication.

Step 2

Cody receives instruction in a self-contained special education classroom and is accessing the enrolled grade-level curriculum through prerequisite skills. The class could be described as implementing an alternate curriculum aligned to alternate achievement standards. Content must be significantly modified and scaffolded to a basic level in order to provide him meaningful access to the curriculum. Cody's curriculum, however, is still aligned to his enrolled grade level. It is still academic in nature rather than wholly functional.

Might Cody require a curriculum that focuses on functional skills in addition to academics? Certainly that should be a consideration, just as remediation and compensation are, but a functional curriculum does not supersede Cody's right to have a curriculum aligned to his enrolled grade level with age-appropriate materials. For students who are older, providing baby toys (e.g., infant rattles), age-inappropriate resources (e.g., nursery rhymes), and reinforcement that is not at the student's functional level (e.g., animated videos) is inappropriate.

Methodologies that Cody requires include systematic and repeated exposure to content. He requires continuous prompting (e.g., verbal, visual, and physical) to remain engaged in a learning task. Video modeling and positive reinforcement are also effective strategies used with him.

Delivery of instruction for Cody will likely be one-on-one when he is acquiring a skill. He can participate in group activities, but direct instruction must include repeated trials with reinforcement consistently provided. Students with multiple disabilities often have many service providers. All providers should work together to determine the delivery of instruction that is most appropriate for Cody and provide it consistently. Because his response repertoire is limited due to his disability, he should be given choices and the opportunity to respond throughout instruction and during the school day to ensure his active participation.

Step 3

The description of Cody's present levels of academic achievement and functional performance in his IEP should be sufficiently detailed so that his academic, functional, and medical needs are understood and the baseline of his current abilities is established. Progress for students like Cody may be incremental. There will be progress when the specially designed instruction he requires is provided. The documentation of current performance must be detailed and accurate so that the progress that Cody makes can be recognized and documented.

DISCUSSION AND RECOMMENDATIONS

Special education does not take the place of the general education curriculum and it does not provide a justification for lowering expectations for students with disabilities. Special education is specially designed instruction. It involves adaptations to content, methodology, and/or delivery of instruction that a student requires as a result of an identified disability. Furthermore, it enables the student to meet the same educational standards that apply to all children.

Specially designed instruction is at the heart of fairness in education. The goal is for students with disabilities to meet the same educational standards that apply to all children. This requires that educators understand each student's disability and the unique needs that arise from it. It requires careful consideration of how the disability impacts access and progress in the general education curriculum. It also requires developing programs that are truly individualized and tailored to meet the student's needs arising from the disability.

Applying the SDI framework detailed in this chapter is hard work. It is time-consuming. It takes vision for school districts to maintain high standards for both students and teachers. It takes courage to do something different and to hold people accountable to implement the programs that are developed. It takes ongoing commitment from all stakeholders. Doing these things consistently and with fidelity will result in better outcomes for students with disabilities, which is truly a matter of social justice.

REFERENCES

Archer, A. L., & Hughes, C. A. (2010). *Explicit instruction: Effective and efficient teaching.* New York: The Guilford Press.

Blum, G., Wilson, M., & Patish, Y. (2015). Moving toward a more socially just classroom through teacher preparation for inclusion. *Catalyst: A Social Justice Forum, 5(1).* Retrieved from http://trace.tennessee.edu/catalyst/vol5/iss1/4/

Center for Applied Special Technology. (2011). *Universal design for learning guidelines version 2.0.* Wakefield, MA: Author.

Center on Education Policy. (2009). *State Test Score Trends Through 2007-08, Part 4: Has progress been made in raising achievement for students with disabilities?* Washington, DC: Author.

Dehn, M. J. (2008). *Working memory and academic learning: Assessment and intervention.* Hoboken, NJ: Wiley.

Feifer, S. G., & De Fina, P. A. (2000). *The neuropsychology of reading disorders: Diagnosis and intervention workbook.* Middletown, MD: School Neuropsych Press, LLC.

Hettleman, K. R. (2013). *Students with disabilities can succeed! How the Baltimore city public schools are transforming special education.* Baltimore, MD: Abell Foundation.

Individuals with Disabilities Education Improvement Act of 2004, Part B, 34 C.F.R. § 300 (Electronic Code of Federal Regulations, 2016).

IRIS Center for Training Enhancements. (2004). Accessing the general education curriculum: Inclusion considerations for students with disabilities. Retrieved from http://iris.peabody.vanderbilt.edu/agc/chalcycle.htm

Jorgensen, C. (2005). The least dangerous Assumption: A challenge to create a new paradigm. *Disability Solutions, 6*(3). Retrieved from http://www.deaccessproject. org/wp-content/uploads/2012/03/Least-Dangerous-Assumption-by-C-Jorgensen.pdf

Mascolo, J. T., Alfonso, V. C., & Flanagan, D. P. (2014). *Essentials of planning, selecting, and tailoring interventions for unique learners.* Hoboken, NJ: Wiley.

McLaughlin, M. J. (2005). *Putting it all together: Providing access to the general education curriculum and meeting the accountability challenge.* Presented at the VCASE Spring Conference. Retrieved from http://www.vcase.org/Pieces/SP05/McLaughlinVCASE05.pdf

National Reading Panel. (2000) Report of the National Reading Panel–Teaching children to read: An evidence-based assessment of the scientific research literature on reading and its implications for reading instruction. Washington, DC: National Institute of Child Health and Human Development.

Nolet, V., & McLaughlin, M. J. (2005). *Accessing the general curriculum: Including students with disabilities in standards-based reform* (2nd ed.). Thousand Oaks, CA: Corwin Press.

Region 4 Education Service Center. (2016). *Standards-based IEP process: Presenter training manual.* Houston: Region 4 Education Service Center.

U.S. Department of Education. (2015). Dear Colleague Letter on Free Appropriate Public Education. Retrieved from http://www2.ed.gov/policy/speced/guid/idea/memosdcltrs/guidance-on-fape-11-17-2015.pdf

Texas Education Agency. (2015). Individualized education program (IEP) annual goal development question and answer document. Retrieved from http://esc20.net/agcnetwork

Thurlow, M. L., Quenemoen, R. F., & Lazarus, S. S. (2011). *Meeting the needs of special education students: Recommendations for the Race to the Top consortia and states.* Minneapolis, MN: National Center on Education Outcomes.

Twachtman-Cullen, D., & Twachtman-Bassett, J. (2011). *The IEP from A to Z: How to create meaningful and measurable goals and objectives.* San Francisco: Jossey-Bass.

Snyder, T. D., de Brey, C., & Dillow, S. A. (2016). *Digest of Education Statistics 2014 (NCES 2016-006).* National Center for Education Statistics, Institute of Education Sciences, U.S. Department of Education. Washington, DC.

Wormeli, R. (2006). *Fair isn't always equal: Assessing and grading in the differentiated classroom.* Portland, ME: Stenhouse.

Chapter 8

RTI: RESPONSE TO INTERVENTION OR RUSHING TO IDENTIFY?

Jannette Reyes

INTRODUCTION

Children living in poverty, children of color, and children who are English Language Learners are more likely to be referred to special education services (e.g., Artiles, Harry, Reschly, & Chinn, 2002; Fernandez & Inserra, 2013). These groups may experience higher rates of risk factors (e.g., hunger, stress, and less exposure to learning opportunities at home) that can contribute to actual learning and behavioral differences. When schools have disproportionately large groups of at-risk students, remediation is often the initial strategy, rather than pre-referral intervention (Rothstein, 2013). This problem is widespread: Three quarters of primary teachers may either not feel qualified or do not feel the responsibility to teach at-risk students (Allington, 2011). Instead, teachers may wait for these students to fail so that they can refer them for special education services, thereby shifting responsibility for these children's education to someone else. The "wait-to-fail" mindset underlies many special education referrals for students suspected of having a specific learning disability. This mindset is compounded by the use of outdated prereferral processes and a lack of consistency and fidelity in general education instruction (Haager, 2007).

These issues raise serious questions about the quality of instruction and intervention practices in some of America's schools, particularly in schools that serve children living in the most vulnerable and underresourced communities, including those where languages other than English are spoken. To address concerns about students who are underprepared for school but who do not require special education services, many school districts have put their trust in the Response to Intervention (RTI) framework. Indeed, RTI has been called "our last, best hope" in education (Scherer, 2010, p. 7). RTI is a multitiered school improvement model led by general education that provides for on-going support for all teachers so that student academic and behavioral difficulties can be prevented. The RTI framework includes the use of culturally responsive, linguistically appropriate, evidence-based instruction, assessment, and interventions, paired with the systemic use of readily available data for daily instructional decision-making and problem-solving. The RTI framework has numerous potential benefits for students who require quality academic, behavioral, and social-emotional supports. However, RTI is only effective if it is implemented correctly and fairly, as various RTI research outcomes have demonstrated (e.g., Balu et al., 2015; Fletcher & Vaughn, 2009).

Although there is not a universal definition of Response to Intervention, the National Joint Committee on Learning Disabilities (2005) provides the following:

> [The RTI model] is generally understood to include multiple tiers that provide a sequence of programs and services for students showing academic difficulties. Briefly, Tier 1 provides high-quality instruction and behavioral supports in general education, Tier 2 provides more specialized instruction for students whose performance and rate of progress lag behind classroom peers, and Tier 3 provides comprehensive evaluation by a multidisciplinary team to determine if the student has a disability and is eligible for special education and related services. (p. 14)

In recent years, much has been written about RTI and recommended phases and scale-up efforts involved in implementation (Center on Instruction, 2008; Kratochwill, Volpiansky, Clements, & Ball, 2007; National Association of State Directors of Special Education, 2008; Sylvester, Lewis, & Severance, 2011). Although there is an abundance of readily-accessible guidance on RTI implementation, school leaders and teaching staff continue to struggle to understand the basic principles of the RTI framework. Perhaps they do not understand the technical language of RTI, have not received proper training on RTI, or simply do not care to know about RTI. Although lack of knowledge about RTI and lack of interest in RTI are themselves problematic, there is a far more challenging problem. Some schools across the country claim to be "doing RTI"; however, disorganized implementation practices have led to a process that has been reduced to filling out stacks of forms and "RTI-ing students," "putting students *in* RTI," and waiting to provide needed services until the student has been "RTI-ed." Furthermore, according to Klinger (2008), there is a lack of culturally responsive practices in most schools' RTI processes. Together, these factors create a breeding ground for social injustice.

BACKGROUND

Capacity-building

In educational terms, capacity-building can be equated with professional development. Professional development is defined as "learning activities related to enhancing skills needed to successfully meet the expectations of one's occupation" (Kratochwill et al., p. 621). Kratochwill and colleagues further note that effective professional development should result in changes in the knowledge and skills that teachers acquire to positively impact student learning. Professional development in RTI has been woefully lacking, resulting in the ongoing use of ineffective prereferral procedures under the guise of RTI.

Prior to the Individuals with Disabilities Education Improvement Act (IDEIA) of 2004, schools used prereferral procedures for identifying students in need of specialized instruction. These prereferral structures took on various names at the campus level, such as Student Assistance Team (SAT), Teacher Assistance Team (TAT), or School-Wide Assistance Team (SWAT). The team would meet to discuss possible solutions to the student's academic difficulties. Solutions would be implemented and the outcomes assessed, often with an eye to justifying a referral to special education (Buck, Polloway, Smith-Thomas, & Cook, 2003). The inclusion of RTI language in the No Child Left Behind (NCLB) Act in 2001 and in IDEIA emphasized the use of scientifically-based prereferral interventions, which could reduce the need for special education services. However, many schools' RTI committees have continued to view RTI as a prereferral process, only giving surface level attention to research-based interventions and using data to support a need for special education referral, rather than using the data to inform general education instruction (Kavale & Spaulding, 2008).

Due to a lack of teacher training and understanding, RTI practices are often dictated by packets of forms that skim the surface of instructional and behavioral supports, reducing these to checkboxes of "interventions" and arbitrary assignment of weeks of intervention per tier. These practices keep the school districts in legal compliance but do nothing to examine and improve Tier 1 academic and behavior support practices. Schools whose RTI processes involve engaging in such a "forms-driven" prereferral process rather than focusing on improving instruction for all students are not engaging in best practices. RTI implementation has been reduced to forms purchased from vendors, paired with vendor-provided "RTI training" consisting primarily of training school staff on how to fill out forms while failing to emphasize the importance of the elements of Tier 1, or core instructional and behavioral support systems. The only beneficiary of these practices is the vendor.

The lack of RTI knowledge among teachers is mirrored by school leaders, who are often unable to articulate the basic ideas and principles of the RTI framework and often delegate the responsibility of leading RTI to an individual who has little knowledge of the purpose or methods of RTI. This individual is offered little to no training in RTI and lacks the autonomy and support needed to initiate the necessary changes to make an impact on the system. Often this person works in isolation, with competing or stalling directives given by other central office and campus-level administrators. The districts have too many administrators who function in centralized, hierarchical, and rule-bound systems that do not support collaborative efforts with school based leadership (Vera, 2009). Often, the lack of consensus at the district administration level leads to segmentation between departments, with employees influenced more by their professional ties than by their dedication to the district's vision and mission statements and their desire to work for the greater good (Spillane, 1996).

In contrast to this state of affairs, the first component of RTI implementation according to the National Association of State Directors of Special Education (2008) blueprints is consensus building, which creates a unified purpose for all school stakeholders. The effective use of RTI reduces special education referrals and increases the quality of general education services. "By retaining more students in general education, RTI reduces the number of students who are faced with the stigma of a 'special education' classification" (Steinberg, 2013, pp.

406–407). However, without a support system of consensus, the district-level RTI leadership is limited in harnessing the power of a collective vision (Kukic, n.d.). Due to a systemic lack of understanding of the RTI framework by school-level and district-level leadership, exacerbated by a lack of a common vocabulary of RTI, schools use "rush-to-identify" practices guided by pseudo-interventions, which result in low response to an intervention by students and an overreliance on the use of forms (Reyes, 2015).

Rush-to-identify practices occur when teachers go through the motions of providing interventions as part of paperwork requirements set forth by their district's special education department. Often these interventions are not research-based, lack integrity, and are carried out for a short amount of time. District level RTI forms offer minimal guidance for teachers on the required intervention periods. For example, the RTI forms might indicate that the intervention must be applied for a designated number of weeks, such as six to eight weeks or eight to twelve weeks. Rush-to-identify practices occur when teachers use the lesser of the weeks required (such as six weeks) and create a new timeline, such as three to six weeks. McCook (2009) refers to this as the "min/max" strategy, wherein the district-level RTI guidance for the minimum number of weeks becomes the maximum and a new minimum term for intervention is created. When a student does not improve during this short timeframe, the teacher interprets this as justification for seeking Tier 3 intervention and refers the student for evaluation.

Campus leaders who have not established buy-in to the RTI framework, or who are highly concerned about state assessment scores, may also promote rush-to-identify practices. Campus leaders feel forced to make decisions on where to place their strongest teachers, either in the primary grades where children are learning to read versus in the grades that are tested and "count" in state accountability. These staffing practices leave the primary grades vulnerable to potentially low-quality instruction and create a group of learners who still lack basic reading skills when they reach the secondary grade levels. Administrative decisions that do not reflect the recommended practices of RTI implementation result in a greater number of students requiring remediation instruction. This creates a funnel effect wherein teachers simply go through the motions in "RTI-ing" students instead of focusing on Tier 1 efforts. As Noll (2013) has noted, "Thirty minutes of intervention can't make up for poor classroom instruction during the other five to six hours of the school day" (p. 57).

Teachers report that they have received little to no training on the basic components of RIT or in the processes required in RTI implementation (Buffum, Mattos, & Weber, 2010; Castro-Villarreal, Rodriguez, & Moore, 2014; Kratochwill et al., 2007; Reyes, 2015). Teachers are then bound by their district and school policies to implement research-based instructional and behavioral interventions with little or no guidance from school leaders. Often the task of leading RTI is delegated to the district office of special education rather than being led by the curriculum and instruction department. These practices send a message to teachers and campus leaders that RTI is a "special ed. thing" rather than an initiative led by general education. The research community promotes these paradigms, as a large percentage (89%) of RTI-related research is published in special education and psychology journals (McDaniel, Albritton, & Roach, 2013). McDaniel and colleagues have also found that the majority of RTI research has focused on Tier 2 (57%), Tier 3 (23%), and progress monitoring in these tiers (64%), rather than on core instruction.

In the absence of research guidance and without proper training, counselors, assistant principals, or even special education personnel are hard-pressed to field questions by teachers seeking support. Through no fault of their own, the best these professionals can do is to offer guidance in how to fill out RTI forms or packets. Some teachers are beacons of light on a sinking ship, and these teachers truly seek solutions for assisting students who struggle. Other teachers have grown to detest RTI in general. Still others have become indifferent to the practices and choose to fly under the radar and do not bother filling out the packets of forms. These misguided practices suggest low teacher efficacy, which can lead to an increase in referrals for special education testing (Soodak & Podell, 1993), rather than a concentrated focus by instructional leaders to evaluate the quality of Tier 1, or core instruction. In many schools, the focus of RTI implementation has shifted from supporting teachers on how to proactively plan for learners' needs and provide engaging instruction and behavioral positive supports in Tier 1, to "RTI-ing" students as a means of "getting help" for struggling learners. When school leaders fail to take an active role in RTI implementation and capacity-building, instructional and behavioral intervention fidelity are compromised. If RTI succeeds it is because of the principal. If RTI fails, it is also because of the principal (McCook, 2009).

In short, rush-to-identify practices result when school systems fail to break with the status quo and engage in First-Order Change thinking processes (Waters, Marzano, & McNulty, 2004). The reluctance to shift to new practices may be due in part to campus leaders who perceive that all struggling learners require specialized instruction or leaders who have biases against certain groups of children (e.g., children of color, children living in single-parent homes, or children whose primary language is one other than English). Such leaders may be less inclined to establish fair and just RTI processes.

Best practice in RTI involves managing the transformation of culture and climate and the use of data to change hearts and minds. For schools to move from status quo to high-quality practices in RTI, leaders must engage in Second Order Change practices, which are nonlinear and recursive in nature, leaving school leaders in a state of disequilibrium (Waters et al., 2004). The status quo of a system is challenged when change initiatives involve a break from the past. RTI cannot be presented to school staff as the next best thing or as an update from their current practices. Schools not prepared to break with the status quo risk presenting RTI as new wine in an old wineskin (McCook, 2009). Response to Intervention implementation without building infrastructure and school staff capacity is itself an act of social injustice for students and for teachers alike.

Treatment Fidelity

Related to the issue of insufficient capacity building is the fidelity of treatment interventions. Fidelity in RTI is defined as "using the curriculum and instructional practices consistently and accurately, as they were intended to be used" (Mallard, 2010, p. 3). Fidelity must be defined and monitored at each tier and phase of implementation. For example, district level leaders must define core, or Tier 1 instruction, and ensure that all teachers have the appropriate training, resources, and materials to effectively implement Tier 1. When teachers lack the appropriate levels of guidance, training, time, and materials, instruction will be compromised.

When districts have failed to build capacity through professional development, they have laid the groundwork for poorly implemented interventions. The result is deficient instruction for struggling students and a possible delay in specially designed instruction. A lack of written policies and procedures at the school district level will result in teachers being unsure of when a student should remain in a certain tier or should be referred for a full and individual evaluation. Teachers reportedly lose motivation and experience low self-efficacy resulting from students' lack of response to interventions. This has important implications, as Castro-Villarreal and colleagues (2014) have found "a strong relation between teacher self-efficacy and indicators of RTI effectiveness. Specifically, [researchers] found that increased understanding and knowledge of RTI led to improved intervention outcomes, satisfaction with results, increased collaboration in teams, and increased data-based decision-making" (p. 105). Teachers who have confidence in their ability to make an impact on student learning are more likely to persist in their efforts; consequently, high fidelity levels are achieved. When teachers experience success in their instruction and intervention, they are more likely to buy in to implementation policies and procedures. In short, success breeds success.

The importance of RTI fidelity is regularly noted in school psychology research studies and is acknowledged by school psychology personnel but is often neither measured nor monitored (Keller-Margulis, 2012). For example, a review of intervention plans (McCook, 2006) found that 85 percent of the time the behavioral definition was undefined. Ninety percent of the time, data was not provided prior to an intervention, and 85 percent of the time a written intervention plan was not found. Furthermore, in 95 percent of the cases reviewed, the interventions were not monitored and no changes were made. When systemic procedures are not established in a district, individual campuses are left to their own devices. Some teachers do the best that they can by properly filling out the forms in efforts to get some assistance for their struggling learners, while other teachers impose their biases and position of power to segregate students who do not fit the perception of normal. The widely accepted paradigm by some educators that parents of low income, racial or ethnic minority, or of second language learners do not care about their child's education (e.g., DeCastro-Ambrosetti & Cho, 2005) becomes the basis for these segregation practices. These educators are quick to place external blame for students' poor academic achievement or behavioral concerns while internal credit readily is accepted by the same educators when students do well in school.

Ensuring fidelity at all levels of implementation may result in stronger feelings of self-efficacy by teachers but will not remediate the deficit perspective held by some. School districts have a responsibility to ensure fidelity of practices by establishing an interdisciplinary team of leaders who communicate with one another on a regular basis. Fidelity requires providing guidance and support to campus-level administrators to assist them in leading RTI efforts and ensuring sustained and quality practices. When schools rush to implement RTI, they neglect to establish a comprehensive plan that includes professional development for school leaders, teachers, and parents, a communication plan (resulting in variations of implementation across the same school district), short-term and long-term implementation goals, and a plan for evaluating fidelity and outcomes of implementation.

CASE STUDY

Jeremy was a fourth-grade student in Mrs. Garcia's class who was struggling in reading. Mrs. Garcia filled out an RTI Packet to refer Jeremy for special education services. Upon review of the school's RTI Packets, it was determined that five other students from Mrs. Garcia's class were also showing signs of academic struggle and had been referred for special education testing. The RTI Packets from Mrs. Garcia's class were examined, beginning with Jeremy's packet. It appeared that reading worksheet pages were listed as part of Jeremy's interventions, and there was a lack of research-based interventions. None of the packets from Mrs. Garcia's class included progress monitoring data.

Three of the six student packets reviewed from Mrs. Garcia's class were associated with English Language Learners (ELL), and all students were failing reading for one or more six- week periods. Jeremy was among these students. A meeting was convened to discuss the findings. The attendees included the school principal, Mr. Barry, Mrs. Garcia, and some district level administrators. At the meeting it was determined that one-third of Mrs. Garcia's class was being referred for special education services. She reported that the previous year she had referred six students who all qualified under the label of Specific Learning Disability (SLD). As of the meeting date, Mrs. Garcia had already referred two additional students who qualified for special education services under the label of SLD, and she was waiting on the results of testing on the six students, including Jeremy.

The principal said Mrs. Garcia was one of his best teachers, who knew how to "spot students who have something wrong with them." Aside from Mrs. Garcia's six RTI Packets, the district level administrators found a file cabinet drawer half-full of more RTI Packets from the campus, and Mr. Barry wanted to know how soon this group of students could be tested so he could "clean house of those students."

Mr. Barry had verbalized his lack of support for the RTI Process during staff meetings and via emails to his teachers. Training and support had been offered to Mr. Barry for his campus by district level administrators, and Mr. Barry continuously refused the support. In an email sent to his teachers immediately following the aforementioned meeting, Mr. Barry instructed his staff to "pull back on instruction in the classroom" with the students who have an RTI packet on file so that there would be "proof" that the struggling students needed testing. Indeed, Mr. Barry was reported to have accused teachers of "helping [struggling] students too much" in the general education setting.

This school is one of the lowest performing schools in the district, is a Title I school, and has one of the highest referral rates for special education testing. There is no interdisciplinary team at the district level, nor are there written policies that guide stakeholders in RTI implementation. After the campus visit to this school, a meeting was requested with the district's Director for Curriculum and Instruction. The director declined a request for a meeting and stated, "We do not have the time right now to think about implementing RTI because our superintendent told us we have to focus on aligning curriculum and improving instruction." Jeremy and the others students who have an active RTI folders in this school district are examples of children who are instructional casualties that are occurring in America's schools.

DISCUSSION AND RECOMMENDATIONS

School leaders have not built capacity for understanding the purpose and principles of RTI. Leaders like Mr. Barry's are dangerous to RTI implementation. Mr. Barry firmly supports referrals to special education and does not understand RTI well enough to establish fidelity of implementation and intervention practices. Teachers like Mrs. Garcia have perfected the process of filling out RTI forms to "RTI students." *RTIing* students has become synonymous with wait-to-fail models prior to IDEIA.

Effective RTI leadership

Schools led by uninformed leaders have rushed into RTI implementation without having a plan *for* implementation. As a result, not all school staff and school leaders have established buy-in, nor are they committed to the process. In many school districts, there is little to no professional development on RTI processes such as universal screening, setting intervention goals, or monitoring student progress. Teachers are receiving little to no guidance from their central office or campus-level administrators, and RTI is perceived as a "new" way to refer students for special education services, rather than as an educational framework in itself. Teachers have grown weary and disillusioned and have lost faith in RTI.

In contrast, school systems where the superintendent of schools and campus principals are leading RTI efforts have had positive results. Such leadership includes a focus on building capacity through hiring highly qualified and highly effective staff, providing professional development, and using data effectively. School leaders who procure highly qualified and highly effective staff in intervention settings yield better results than in settings where a paraprofessional is used (Allington, 2011). RTI implementation has promoted the unpacking of content area standards not only in reading and mathematics but in other content areas as well (Whitaker, 2012). Furthermore, RTI implementation has renewed the need for teacher mentoring and collaboration, paired with quality professional development experiences that move from basic skill acquisition to a focus on ongoing learning structures for teachers, such as professional learning communities (Jimerson, Burns, & VanDerHeyden, 2007). School systems that have included professional development goals in their school improvement plans have a greater probability of "doing RTI right." With regard to RTI's use of data, Engels (2015) cautions that schools must consider multiple measures of data and rule out false positives. Student progress monitoring data is important, but Engels warns against overtesting students.

However, knowledge of curriculum and instruction, support of professional development, and appropriate use of data are not enough for school district level administrators to prepare to lead in the RTI world. School district-level administrators must view RTI implementation as synonymous with school improvement. To achieve such improvement, district-level administrators should ensure a common vocabulary is understood, that resources are properly allocated, and that hiring practices reflect the goals and vision of RTI (Kratochwill et al., 2007). It is essential that school leaders create a culture that views RTI as the primary mode of functioning on which all other initiatives are built, versus as an optional add-on to the daily functioning of school practices. Leadership in RTI requires reflective practices, and leaders must be willing to take a step back and research answers to questions rather than risk misinforming principals or teachers.

Furthermore, the practice of assigning one person to "be *in charge* of RTI," instead of assembling a district-level team with representative membership, increases the likelihood that rush-to-identify practices will occur. It is unfeasible for one person assigned at the school district level to understand the academic, linguistic, behavioral, and social-emotional needs of at-risk students in addition to understanding best practices in curriculum alignment, instructional adaptations, and assessment practices. Similarly, expecting fast-paced implementation is unrealistic. Quality RTI implementation takes four to six years for full implementation to occur. Full implementation includes "policy and regulatory change, staff development, and development of building/ district-based procedures" (Batche, 2006, Slide number 45).

Effective RTI Implementation

Six reputable organizations have described the recommended phases of RTI implementation. The results shown in Table 8.1 clearly indicate that school leaders must consider certain actions prior to implementation. Leaders must explore options, develop a plan, create awareness of the plan and of the RTI framework, establish buy-in, and build capacity, and *then* engage in RTI implementation. Leadership must know the difference between RTI awareness training and RTI implementation efforts. Awareness training is simply informing staff of the *what* of RTI, whereas implementation training must be on-going and emphasize the *why* and the *how* of RTI.

An abundance of research has examined various types of professional development and effects on student achievement. Although many would argue that more funds are needed to provide quality training to teachers, the return on professional development is often dismal and riddled with piecemealed practices leading to arbitrary and haphazard planning for teacher learning (Moore, Kochan, Kraska, &

Table 8.1
PHASES OF RESPONSE TO INTERVENTION IMPLEMENTATION

Center on Instruction (2008) http://www.rtictrl.org/levels. php	*National Association of State Directors of Special Education (2008)* http://www.nasdse.org/ Portals/0/DISTRICT.pdf	*McCook (2009)*
• Exploration • Installation • Initial Implementation • Full Implementation • Innovation • Sustainability	• Consensus Building • Infrastructure Building • District Level Implementation	• Awareness • Commitment • Capacity • Implementation • Evaluation
RtI Action Network (2011) http://www.rtinetwork.org/ getstarted	*National Center on Response to Intervention (2011)* http://www.rti4success.org/	*Meadows Center for Preventing Educational Risk; University of Texas System/ Texas Education Agency (2010)* http://buildingrti.utexas.org/ leadership-tools/ rti-implementation-flowchart

• Build Support
• Develop a Plan
• Implement Your Plan
• Evaluate and Refine Implementation
	• Exploring and Adopting
	• Planning
	• Implementing
	• Continuously Improving
		1-Getting Started
		  • Build Campus Commitment and Form Leadership Team
		  • Conduct Needs Assessment
		  • Develop Campus Action Plan
		2-Implementing RtI
		  • Implement Campus Action Plan
		3-Monitoring Implementation
		  • Review Progress and Revise Campus Action Plan

Reames, 2011). Most schools that receive an increase in resources fail to use the new dollars in strategic ways to improve student performance (Odden & Picus, 2011). According to the Center for Public Education (2013), it takes on average 20 separate opportunities for teachers to practice a new skill before that skill is mastered. This number of practice instances increases as the complexity of the new skill increases. Professional development, including both training and multiple opportunities for guided practice, is a vital and often neglected component of RTI implementation. Instead, teachers are expected to follow an ambiguous set of internal procedures and processes that leave them feeling isolated and disillusioned.

The thrust of *school improvement* should be *people* improvement. Those who have worked in the field of education long enough would understand that the pendulum of educational reform is often accompanied with "new and improved" educational rhetoric such as, *rigor, data-based decision making, research-based instruction, learning styles,* and *higher order thinking.* No matter how the reform is packaged, teachers are not buying it without adequate support and resources. Teachers may sit politely and patiently in professional development sessions, secretly checking and updating their social networks or responding to text messages, and all the while the leadership that requested the training has left the building and perhaps returns at the end of the training day. In defense of the teachers, if the leadership fails to demonstrate an active interest in the topic, the message is clear to the teachers: This is not important and this, too, shall pass. In addition, for teachers to truly master research-based interventions, on-going coaching and feedback opportunities must be provided. Work by Timperley, Wilson, Barrar, and Fung (2008) as well as Calderón (1999) indicates that when teachers receive on-going support and feedback while engaging in professional learning communities (PLCs), teachers report higher rates gains of knowledge, skill, and use. These learning formats are associated with a large improvement in student achievement: 1.68 standard deviations. These kinds of improvements are worth investing in.

To communicate the importance of RTI for a campus and/or district, leadership should select an organizational framework such as those included in Table 8.1, and research then establish an action plan for each phase of implementation. The organizational framework serves as a road map, and the leaders must be willing to share the driver's seat in efforts to move their district along in the process. When leadership is not directly involved in RTI implementation and procedures and processes are not established, both capacity-building and fidelity issues are likely to occur.

Effective RTI Collaboration

RTI requires a joint effort between general and special education (Galvin, 2007). Possible solutions include establishing an interdisciplinary RTI guidance committee at the district level for the purpose of establishing district-wide guidelines for all staff, including district- and campus-level leaders, and for teachers. A starting point for school districts is to engage in a root-cause analysis, using the results to design a professional development plan for all levels of stakeholders to build capacity. Furthermore, school districts should follow the proposed activities and actions in the *RTI Implementation Blueprints* provided by the National Association of State Directors of Special Education (2008). Data should be used from students who are evaluated for special education services but who do not qualify (DNQ), to inform and adjust instructional and behavioral support interventions at Tier 1. School systems engage in the blame game: "If only the elementary campuses would do their job" and "If only the parents would do their job." RTI implementation will require that school leaders reflect on the outcomes of their own polices, processes, and practices, examine multiple sources of data, and ask tough questions. Rather than asking why the student is failing in their system, school district administrators should ask why the *system* is failing the student.

To evaluate RTI collaboration and implementation efforts at least two times a year, school districts can use *The Outcomes-Driven Model* (Kaminski & Cummings, 2008) as a guide. This model asks four questions: What is happening? Why is it happening? How can we fix it? Did we fix it? This cyclical model of system review ensures that RTI implementation stays on the right track and no assumptions are made about the quality of practices, so that the system does not stray towards its natural tendency of relying on the RTI forms or on subjective data on which to base decisions.

Future Directions

The bad news is that RTI practices may quite possibly be phased out in the next few years. The good news is that the "mother ship" of RTI is coming. This "mother ship," also known as the Multi-Tiered Systems of Support, or MTSS, will have its own share of promises. Approximately 40 states in the nation have made the transition from RTI to MTSS. The MTSS framework differs from RTI in MTSS's greater focus on collaborative efforts at all tiers of the system. Namely, district-level leaders will commit to defining programs, policies, and practices at the district, school, and classroom levels. Additionally, a greater focus on collaboration between special education and general education will be promoted as part of the MTSS model. Professional development and leadership will take center stage, and the social and emotional needs of students will be as important as the academic and behavioral needs (Hurst, 2014). The benefits of MTSS decision making will include the use of reliable and timely data, correctly interpreting the data, and making meaningful instructional changes as needed. Evaluation will be built into all tiers to ensure that the micro and macro components of the system are working. The primary question in the MTSS system will be, "Is the core instruction working?" (Metcalf, n.d.).

Capacity-building is not a new concept. Neither are the topics of fidelity of implementation or quality leadership. Educated professionals have all the knowledge to improve conditions in schools, but there is one question: Are they *willing* to do so? When shortcuts are taken, students may be harmed as a result. In Response to Intervention, there are no shortcuts. Social justice calls for us to challenge inequity, value diversity, eliminate discrimination, and advocate for change. RTI cannot simply exist on paper. Unless strong and effective school leaders ramp up capacity efforts and establish measures of fidelity in RTI, students like Jeremy will continue to flounder in at-risk settings, ignored by teachers like Mrs. Garcia and discounted by principals like Mr. Barry.

REFERENCES

Allington, R. L. (2011). What at-risk readers need. *Educational Leadership, 68*(6), 40–45.

Artiles, A. J., Harry, B., Reschly, D. J., & Chinn, P. C. (2002). Over-identification of students of color in special education: A critical overview. *Multicultural Perspectives, 4*(1), 3–10.

Balu, R., Zhu, P., Doolittle, F., Schiller, E., Jenkins, J., & Gersten, R. (2015). *Evaluation of response to intervention practices for elementary school reading*. Washington, DC: National Center for Educational Evaluation and Regional Assistance.

Batche, G. M. (2006, January). *Problem solving and response to intervention: Implications for state and district policies and practices*. Paper session presented at the meeting of the Council for Advancement and Support of Education.

Buck, G. H., Polloway, E. A., Smith-Thomas, A., & Cook, K. W. (2003). Pre-referral intervention processes: A survey of state practices. *Exceptional Children, 69*(3), 349–360.

Buffum, A., Mattos, M., & Weber, C. (2010). The why behind RTI. *Educational Leadership, 68*(2), 10–16.

Calderón, M. (1999). Teachers learning communities for cooperation in diverse settings. *Theory into Practice, 38*(2), 94–99.

Castro-Villarreal, F., Rodriguez, B. J., & Moore, S. (2014). Teacher' perceptions and attitudes about response to intervention (RTI) in their schools: A qualitative analysis. *Teaching and Learning Education, 40*, 104–112.

Center on Instruction. (2008). RTI classification tool and resource locator. Retrieved from http://www.rtictrl.org/levels.php

DeCastro-Ambrosetti, D., & Cho, G. (2005). Do parents value education? Teachers' perceptions of minority parents. *Multicultural Education, 13*(2), 44–46.

Engels, K. (2015). RTI: What teachers know that computers don't. *Educational Leadership, 73*(3), 72–76.

Fernandez, N., & Inserra, A. (2013). Disproportionate classification of ESL students in U.S. special education. *TESL-EJ, 17*(2), 1–22.

Fletcher, J. M., & Vaughn, S. (2009). Response to intervention: Preventing and remediating academic difficulties. *Child Development Perspectives, 3*(1), 30–37.

Galvin, M. (2007). Feature article: Implementing response to intervention (RTI): Considerations for practitioners. Retrieved from http://jupiter.plainedgeschools. org/district/uploads/Implementing%20RtI%20Considerations%20for%20Practitioners.pdf

Haager, D. (2007). Promises and cautions regarding using response to intervention with English language learners. *Learning Disability Quarterly, 30*, 213–218.

Hurst, S. (2014, January 06). What is the difference between RTI and MTSS? [Blog post]. Retrieved from http://www.readinghorizons.com/blog/ what-is-the-difference-between-rti-and-mtss

Individuals with Disabilities Education Improvement Act of 2004, 34 C.F.R. § 300.8 (Electronic Code of Federal Regulations, 2016).

Jimerson, S. R., Burns, M. K., & VanDerHeyden, A. M. (2007). *Handbook of response to intervention: The science and practice of assessment and intervention.* New York: Springer Science+Business Media, LLC.

Kaminski, R. A., & Cummings, K. D. (2008). Linking assessment to instruction: Using dynamic indicators of basic early literacy skills in an outcome driven model. *Dynamic Measurement Group.* Retrieved from https://dibels.org/papers/PM_ BDA_032708.pdf

Kavale, K. A., & Spaulding, L. S. (2008). Is Response to Intervention good policy for specific learning disability? *Learning Disabilities Research & Practice, 23*(4), 169–179.

Keller-Margulis, M. (2012). Fidelity of implementation framework: A critical need for response to intervention models . *Psychology in Schools, 49*(4), 342–352.

Klingner, J. (2008, July 3). Response to Intervention. [Blog post.] Retrieved from http://www.niusileadscape.org/bl/response-to-intervention-rti/#more-20

Kratochwill, T. R., Volpiansky, P., Clements, M., & Ball, C. (2007). Professional development in implementing and sustaining multitier prevention models: Implications for response to intervention. *School Psychology Review, 36*(4), 618–631.

Kukic, S. J. (n.d.). Relentlessly doing whatever it takes to sustain the change necessary to improve the achievement of all students. Retrieved from http://www.rtinetwork.org/getstarted/buildsupport/rti-leadership-that-works

Mallard, D. (2010). *Fidelity of implementation within a response to intervention (RTI) framework tools for schools.* Washington, DC: National Center on Response to Intervention.

McCook, J. E. (2006). *The RTI guide: Developing and implementing a model in your schools.* Palm Beach Gardens, GL: LRP Publications.

McCook, J. E. (2009). *Leading and managing RTI: Five steps for building and maintaining the framework.* Palm Beach Gardens, FL: LRP Publications.

McDaniel, S., Albritton, K., & Roach, A. (2013). Highlighting the need for further response to intervention research in general education. *Research in Higher Education Journal, 20,* 1–12. Retrieved from http://eric.ed.gov/?id=EJ1064666

Metcalf, T. (n.d.). What's your plan? Accurate decision making within a multi-tier system of supports: Critical areas in tier 1. Retrieved from http://www.rtinetwork.org/essential/tieredinstruction/tier1/accurate-decision-making-within-a-multi-tier-system-of-supports-critical-areas-in-tier-1

Moore, S. D., Kochan, F. K., Kranska, M., & Reames, E. H. (2011, November 2). Professional development and student achievement in high poverty schools: Making the connection. *International Studies in Educational Administration, 39*(2), 65–79.

National Association of State Directors of Special Education. (2008). *Response to intervention blueprints for implementation district level.* Retrieved from http://www.nasdse.org/Portals/0/DISTRICT.pdf

National Joint Committee on Learning Disabilities. (2005). Responsiveness to intervention and learning disabilities. Retrieved from http://www.ldonline.org/?module=uploads&func=download&fileId=461

No Child Left Behind Act of 2001, Pub. L. No. 107–110. 115 §1425 (2002).

Noll, B. (2013). Seven ways to kill RTI. *Kappan, 94*(6), 55–59.

Odden, A., & Picus, L. (2011). Improving teaching and learning when budgets are tight. *Phi Delta Kappan, 93*(1), 42–48.

Reyes, J. S. (2015). *Assessing elementary teachers' understanding of the language contained in their district's required RTI forms* (Unpublished doctoral dissertation). Argosy University, Online.

Rothstein, R. (2013). Why our schools are segregated. *Educational Leadership, 70*(8), 50–55.

Scherer, M. (2010). Not waiting for superman. *Educational Leadership, 68*(2), 7.

Soodak, L. C., & Podell, D. M. (1993). Teacher efficacy and student problem as factors in special education referral. *Journal of Special Education, 27*(1), 66.

Spillane, J. (1996). School districts matter. *Educational Policy, 10*(1), 63–87.

Steinberg, G. (2013). Amending section 1415 of the IDEA: Extending procedural safeguards to response-to-intervention students. *Columbia Journal of Law and*

Social Problems, 46(3), 393–429.

Sylvester, R., Lewis, S., & Severance, J. (2011). Educators maneuvering the challenges of RTI conferences: Guidelines for success. *Delta Kappa Gamma Bulletin, 78*(2), 27–32.

Timperley, H., Wilson, A., Barrar, H., & Fung, I. (2008). *Teacher professional learning and development.* Auckland, New Zealand: Iterative Best Evidence Synthesis Programme.

Vera, M. C. (2009). *Leading change in schools: Leadership practices for a district supported school-based reform model* (Doctoral dissertation). Retrieved from http://scholarcommons.usf.edu/etd/?utm_source=scholarcommons.usf.edu%2Fetd%2F68&utm_medium=PDF&utm_campaign=PDFCoverPages

Waters, J. T., Marzano, R. J., & McNulty, B. (2004). Leadership that sparks learning. *Educational Leadership, 61*(7), 48–51.

Whitaker, J. R. (2012). Responding to the need for intervention. *Science and Children, 50*(4), 75–79.

CONCLUSION

CATHERINE R. BARBER, HELEN S. SHAW, AND TERA TORRES

The case studies in this book have presented a portrait of many of the injustices that currently plague the special education system. Although each story is unique, the common theme is that children with disabilities do not always receive the educational services and supports that they need to reach their full potential. Having identified some of the major injustices in the system and specific recommendations for addressing them, we conclude with our vision for the next chapter in special education.

RESTORING JUSTICE TO SPECIAL EDUCATION

Appropriate Access to Special Education Services

In 2016, the *Houston Chronicle* began publishing an exposé series, "Denied" (Rosenthal, 2016), based on investigative reporting into special education practices in Texas. The common theme throughout the series was that Texas–the 2nd most populous state in the United States– was consistently *underserving* children with disabilities. Statistics indicated that the percentage of students receiving special education in Texas (8.5%) was substantially lower than the national average (13%) in 2015, and the 8.5% rate was exactly the benchmark that the Texas Education Agency (TEA) had set for special education enrollment many years earlier (Rosenthal, 2016). This disparity between the national and state rates has apparently not been due to the success of Response to Intervention or other efforts to reduce inaccurate referrals and placement in Texas. Rather, story after story revealed systematic denial of services for students who truly required them. The exposé alleged that such denial was a cost-cutting measure and that schools imposed caps on special education enrollment in response to penalties and warnings from TEA (Rosenthal, 2016).

The public outcry over this situation was immediate. The U.S. Department of Education indicated that TEA should halt any cap on special education unless the state could show that this practice did not deny students special education services for which they are eligible (Swenson, 2016). Meanwhile, TEA's Deputy Commissioner of Academics (Schwinn, 2016) systematically denied the accusations in a letter to the Office of Special Education and Rehabilitative Services (OSERS). OSERS began holding listening sessions across the state to better understand the problem, and an investigation was still pending at the time of this book's publication (Ryder, 2017).

It can be challenging to sort out facts from perceptions and opinions in such a complex situation. However, the emotions that families feel when their children do not get the educational services that they require are all too real. Even if local educational agencies have the very best intentions and are making decisions with their constituents' best interests in mind, there are some decisions that should not be left to local authorities. For example, it should not be a local or state agency's role to determine what a disability actually is or the rules by which student need is assessed. The stories in the *Chronicle*'s exposé, like those in this book, suggest that clear, comprehensive definitions and descriptions of disabilities—and research-based evaluation practices—are needed. Such definitions would help to address state-by-state and district-by-district inconsistencies in the application of federal law (Torres, Chapter 1). Otherwise, children will continue to be denied the services that they need due to idiosyncratic identification and evaluation practices.

Such denial of needed services is unjust, irresponsible, and shortsighted. As Torres (Chapter 2) has argued, any costs saved by failing to provide a free appropriate public education to all students will be eventually offset many times over when under-educated students leave school and enter the workforce unprepared (or, worse, fail to enter the workforce at all). In the case of students who fall in the gap due to general learning difficulties, effective special education services must be extended to this population so that they can finish school as educated, productive citizens. In cases where the unserved needs are emotional or behavioral, the cost may be even steeper (Wells, Chapter 3), given the high rates of social maladjustment and emotional disturbance in the criminal justice system (Leone & Weinberg, 2012). As these chapters illustrate, the existing definitions of disability categories (as regulated by IDEA and its reauthorization) are limited in their ability to identify all children who need special services. But even more accurate and extensive definitions of disability are useless if these are ignored by the state and local educational agencies that have been charged with implementing the law.

Appropriate Placement in Special Education

As Porter and Walters (Chapter 4) and Wells and De La Garza (Chapter 5) have demonstrated, the other side of the coin is the *inappropriate* placement of children in special education, which may unjustly deny them full access to the general education curriculum and lead to lowered expectations and negative outcomes (Sullivan & Proctor, 2016). It is imperative that evaluators and other school personnel make every effort to avoid cultural bias, to ensure testing fairness, and to carefully consider other factors contributing to a child's lower achievement. Students who are struggling because of cultural or linguistic differences, inadequate language programming, or environmental disadvantage need support. However, special education should not be the default option for these students.

At the same time, it must be recognized that some students who are environmentally disadvantaged also have diagnosable disabilities. Similarly, some students who lack English proficiency also have disabilities. Although extra care must be taken to ensure that alternative explanations for students' academic struggles are assessed, the presence of factors such as environmental disadvantage and/or cultural and linguistic differences should not be an automatic rule-out for disability diagnosis. Over- and underrepresentation of culturally and linguistically diverse students in special education will continue until educators are better able to check their implicit biases at the door and carefully assess the complex interplay of factors that contribute to a student's performance in school.

The "gatekeepers" of children's access to special education are evaluators. It is our opinion that the requirements for obtaining certification as evaluators must be more stringent. It is not enough to complete a specified amount of fieldwork and pass a licensure or certification exam. Candidates should have a background in special education. As part of certification renewal, evaluators should also be required to engage in reflective practice, including a description of challenging evaluation cases and their rationale for making the decisions that were made.

Improved Results through Evidence-based Practices

Although access is a critical factor in evaluating special education, focusing exclusively on access fails to address an equally or perhaps more problematic issue: The very system to which children have been unjustly denied access is itself broken. Parents may be advocating for their children's placement into a special education system that often does not help them. Despite research that shows that students with disabilities are able to learn with the proper supports (Harr-Robins, et al., 2013), large-scale studies have consistently shown that special education, on average, does not appreciably improve students' academic outcomes (Harr-Robins et al., 2013; Morgan, Frisco, Farkas, & Hibel, 2010; National Center for Learning Disabilities, 2014). In addition, national statistics show a large and persistent performance gap between students with and without disabilities (Harr-Robins et al., 2013). The incongruence of these two findings—that most students with disabilities can learn, but many students with disabilities are not achieving the expected outcomes even when they receive special education services— suggests that current special education practices often do not provide the proper supports for students with disabilities. Of course, there are always exceptions to research findings, and some schools and school districts have highly effective special education programming. However, these laudable success stories should not be seen as a sign that problems do not exist in special education. There continue to be vast disparities in outcomes for students with disabilities.

Why are the results so abysmal? There are no simple answers. Students may fail to progress because of inadequate, rigid, or perfunctory Individualized Educational Programs that do not take into account the child's ability and potential (Staniszewski, Chapter 6). This failure may also be attributed to a lack of understanding and implementation of specially designed instruction, as Ten Napel (Chapter 7) has described. It may stem from the failures of schools to appropriately implement Response to Intervention (RTI) initiatives that use research-based practices at all tiers of assessment and intervention (Reyes, Chapter 8).

Other factors not explored here, such as the underuse of effective co-teaching models (Friend, 2008), overwhelming paperwork (Klein, 2004), and the nation wide shortage of special education teachers (U.S. Department of Education, 2016), are also likely culprits. One thing is clear, however: The inadequacies are not due to widespread lack of care on the part of special educators. The teachers, evaluation staff, and others who work with students with disabilities are often tireless advocates for children. However, even the best, most dedicated educators can fall into learned helplessness in the face of relentless bureaucracy, unsupportive leadership, low pay, and stressful working conditions. These factors must be addressed if special education personnel are to be as effective as possible.

One way of addressing these issues is by substantially investing in evidence-based preservice training and professional development for both special educators and general educators. All teachers need preparation to work with a diverse student body. It is misguided for training programs (whether baccalaureate or alternative teacher certification) to assume that children with disabilities will be taught exclusively or even primarily by a special education teacher. This assumption has been used to justify the failure to teach general education teachers about the needs of this population. Instead, training programs should recognize that all teachers are more effective when they have knowledge and skill in working with students from all backgrounds. Even if general education teachers are not providing specially designed instruction, they should have a solid understanding of the challenges and needs of students with disabilities and how to address these.

In addition, special educators need ongoing professional development that is scientifically sound. There are numerous evidence-based interventions for students in special education, but these are not always adopted or appropriately implemented by school systems (Fletcher, 2015). Schools and districts must resist adopting "trendy" programs simply because these have been well-packaged. Educators need access to the most effective strategies and programs, and they need ongoing support and professional development to hone their skills in evidence-based interventions. Although this will likely require additional funding, it is not enough simply to throw money at the problem. Expenditures should be thoughtful and should fund professional development opportunities that have shown measurable results. Hiring additional special education administrators (rather than additional special education teachers), purchasing assessment and intervention technology that is flashy but not substantiated by evidence, and funding workshops on pedagogical practices that have no research base are not best practices and thus should not be the target of increased special education funding.

Empowering Families

Under IDEIA (2004), parents have well-defined rights. Schools must make reasonable efforts to seek parental consent for evaluation and services (34 CFR §300.300). Parents may seek an independent educational evaluation if they disagree with the school evaluation (34 CFR §300.502). Parents also have the right to file a state complaint if they feel that their child is not receiving appropriate services (34 CFR §300.153). The effectiveness of these and other parental rights in special education depends on parents understanding their rights and knowing how to exercise them. The success of these statutes also requires all parents to have the knowledge and confidence to advocate effectively for their child. However, not all parents enjoy the benefit of a strong education, and some parents may be intimidated by consent forms; highly technical evaluation reports; Admission, Review, and Dismissal meetings; and other points of intersection between the parents and the school's special education program.

Therefore, parents must be empowered in the special education process (Porter & Walters, Chapter 4). Such empowerment includes full disclosure about a school's (and school district's) successes and setbacks in the special education realm. Schools must make concerted efforts to engage parents throughout the special education process. Although parents do have responsibilities for their own participation, numerous barriers to full participation exist; these barriers should not simply be ignored, with lack of parental involvement chalked up to parents "not caring" about their child's education.

This is not to say that parents should completely dictate the terms of their child's IEP or demand access to services that are ineffective. Rather, there must be a partnership between parents and school officials at each stage: referral, evaluation, placement, and service provision. Educators must have greater trust in parents' understanding of their children, and parents must have greater trust in educators' knowledge and expertise. Such trust, however, must be earned.

CHALLENGING THE STATUS QUO

The recommendations in this book have largely focused on solving specific problems within the special education system. They provide short-term solutions to the issues of inconsistent identification processes, inadequate identification categories, disproportionate representation, ill-conceived IEPs, ineffective specially designed instruction, and poorly implemented RTI programs. By advocating for and implementing these recommendations, educational leaders and policymakers can take a substantial step towards correcting the social injustices of special education. Perhaps if these changes were made, the special education system as conceptualized by current education laws would be adequate: Educators would identify some children as having disabilities and therefore special educational needs; these children would receive specially designed instruction in the least restrictive setting with the goal of achieving grade-level standards; and all progress would be measured and documented for parents, school leaders, and lawmakers to review. However, this status quo is based on numerous assumptions: that only children who have a federally-recognized disability need specially designed instruction, that all children should be learning the same thing as the same time, and that progress can be reduced to quantitative measures. When we begin the question these assumptions, then we have no choice but to challenge the status quo.

Meeting All Children's Educational Needs

As a country, we have determined that the major route to social mobility is the power of education. However, we are not really educating all children, as mandated by the original Education for All Handicapped Children Act of 1975 and subsequent legislation. Five decades ago, children whom adults believed could not succeed in the regular classroom were sent to group homes and state hospitals if their parents had the money and kept at home by parents if the family could not afford other options. These children are now ostensibly included in the public school system, but many continue to be underserved due to their special education status. Children continue to be sorted into categories, with those who do not meet adults' expectations referred to a suboptimal system if they are "lucky" enough to have been diagnosed with a disability. Meanwhile, those who do not meet identification criteria (e.g., socially maladjusted students and those with general learning difficulties) are at the mercy of their school. If the school personnel are well-versed in strategies for helping these students and are motivated to do so, then these students will have their educational needs met. But there is no guarantee that this will happen, and in many cases students end up graduating with less knowledge and fewer skills, if they graduate at all.

Recognizing Individual Differences

Society also advances the notions that every child has the same opportunities and that every child has the ability to overcome obstacles ("picking one's self up by the bootstraps," we call it). These notions are consistent with essentialist educational philosophy—the idea that all children should learn the same academic essentials, preferably in the same order and at the same time (Imig & Imig, 2006). However, as our work has shown, children do not have the same opportunities, nor do they share the same struggles.

Problems in public education can be attributed, at least in part, to our trying to put progressivism into an essentialist system. We can tout the "individualized attention" our students receive or the fact that students of all ability levels in are being educated in an "inclusion" classroom. However, the curriculum still requires a predetermined knowledge set, and teachers must adhere to this value system and deposit essential components into the students. Here is where we think our system is sorely wrong. Rather than trying to figure out a way to make all children the same, we should be determining where each child is individually and then take each child however far he or she can go. In an ideal world, we would value all people, and we would provide all people with the necessary skill sets to be active, productive, and happy members of society. Each person's strengths and weaknesses would be assessed, and instruction would challenge those weaknesses while encouraging and cultivating the areas of strength. Such an approach would undoubtedly require a fundamental reconceptualization not only of special education but of general education as well.

Embracing Qualitative Assessment

Children—with or without a disability—learn different subjects at different rates, have strengths and weaknesses in different areas, and have different motivations. However, the uniqueness of each child is often overlooked in the effort to achieve the same standards for all children in all subjects—to show adequate yearly progress on state tests (No Child Left Behind Act of 2001) and thereby avoid penalties. This approach blatantly ignores whether test results say something truly meaningful about a child's ability to thrive in the world. Similarly, IEPs are often reduced to checklists of learning goals that map onto state standards. Rather than truly evaluating a child's progress in the curriculum, schools have become obsessed with demonstrating that students are performing "adequately" on predefined, universal standards.

We propose that rigid grade-level standards and the associated measures of learning are themselves part of the problem. The state standards are treated as unquestionable—if a group of educators and politicians have deemed a list of content areas and skills as "essential," then this list must be correct (and comprehensive). There are some skills and content areas that are universally valuable; however, it is questionable whether a one-size-fits-all curriculum is appropriate. To take one extreme example, the kindergarten-level Texas Essential Knowledge and Skills are summarized in a 29-page document (Texas Education Agency, 2016) that includes such standards as "use data to create real-object and picture graphs" (p. 10); "explain how authority figures make and enforce rules" (p. 16); "identify ways to prevent the transmission of head lice such as sharing brushes and caps" (p. 20); and "comply with acceptable digital safety rules, fair use guidelines, and copyright laws" (p. 29). Although these areas of knowledge and skill are no doubt useful at some point in most people's lives, should they be assessed as an essential part of every five-year-old Texan's education?

This is not to say that standards are unimportant; of course, they are. Without rigorous standards, schools may significantly undereducate students. However, we believe that standards should inform, rather than dictate, the curriculum. Rigid standards-based curricula can give policymakers and others a false sense of security that education is more rigorous simply because it is more codified and more easily assessed for accountability purposes. However, such efforts ignore the fact that teachers and students have individual interests, strengths, and weaknesses. Putting 20 or more unique young personalities into a room with a teacher who has his or her own personality, imposing a single curriculum on all of them, and expecting children to achieve identical results is a fool's errand. This scenario doesn't even take into account that some of these children will have disabilities, disadvantages, and other special educational needs.

We propose an alternative. What if students and teachers first participated in personality matching processes to determine whether those relationships would be conducive to learning? After all, in a truly progressivist system, the teacher "is not in the school to impose certain ideas or to form certain habits in the child . . . [the teacher] is to select the influences which shall affect the child and to assist him in properly responding to these influences" (Dewey, 1897, para. 19). What if each child also participated in extensive aptitude screenings or proclivity inventories to determine what would be taught that semester or that year? Dewey (1897) also tells us, "The child's own instincts and powers furnish the material and give the starting point for all education" (para. 3). Moreover, "Without insight into the psychological structure and activities of the individual, the educative process will . . . be haphazard and arbitrary" (Dewey, 1897, para. 3).

Furthermore, what if the curriculum was allowed to be fluid and constantly changing so that as a child matured and his or her interests and desires changed, so would instruction? What if each child was truly seen as a collection of puzzle pieces, and our job as educators was to help each child put together his or her own pieces? Far from "watering down" the curriculum, this would allow for more meaningful and individualized learning experiences by honoring children's interests and abilities while challenging them to overcome their limitations. In such an educational system, the chief difference between students with and without disabilities would be the type of specially designed instruction they receive, as each student's learning experience would already be unique.

In such a system, learning should be assessed not just with standardized tests but also with qualitative tools such as portfolios, artifacts, interviews, and observation. Qualitative outcomes are often viewed as less trustworthy than quantitative measures, as the latter are easier to interpret and compare across sites. Thus, to earn the public's trust in this realm, educators and administrators would have to demonstrate their commitment to reliable, valid, and meaningful assessment. The focus of accountability would shift away from the assessment of whether students had memorized content based on pre-defined standards and toward whether educators did everything they could to help students thrive and achieve meaningful learning goals. Eisner (1988) once stated, "I hope we will . . . learn how to see what we are not able to describe in words, much less measure" (p. 20). This is our hope for the future of special education—that children receive an education that is specially tailored to their needs, whatever those needs are.

Reflecting on Process, Not Product

How might such changes come about? In reflecting upon this book and the methodological approach used, we have affirmed that we must change the educational course of every child who is struggling within the confines of our current system. There is no room for error—the impact of a mistake on a child's life can be profound, as can be the impact of making the right decision at the right time. We have determined that there is much room for reform within both the special education system and the public education system as a whole. We think much needs to be changed, and for evaluators and special education teachers in particular, these changes include the best form of professional development: reflective practice. Everyone who works with children must regularly spend time reflecting upon their roles within the school and the impact of those roles on themselves and the children—not the impact of those roles on the school.

Reflective practice embraces those of us who use it by requiring us to identify our own value systems and talk through our own biases. It also requires us to own our decisions and hold ourselves accountable. If we were to be held accountable for our own actions and decisions, we believe that we would render those decisions more carefully. Accountability is not simply a matter of test scores. It is a matter of integrity—daily asking oneself, "Did I do the right by the children in my care?"

Many stories end with a moral or a lesson. We have observed two fundamental social justice lessons across the stories in this book: First, when dealing with children, particularly other people's children, we cannot remain distanced; the stakes are simply too high. Second, as educators we must acknowledge, honor, and share the stories of the children with whom we work. It is through this storytelling that we find answers, and telling stories can be used to elicit help for students in an educational system that is exclusionary and convoluted at best. We live in a world where some things are only available to some people, including specialized programming and individualized education. This state of affairs is not compatible with our values, particularly in light of our conceptualization of social justice as involving fairness, recognition, and a voice in the decision-making process (Gewirtz, 2006). Educators, lawmakers, parents, and society in general ultimately want the same thing: a strong educational system that cultivates all students' academic interests and aptitudes, that fosters children's curiosity and love of learning, and that develops the whole child. Students with disabilities should not be left out of this vision. Social justice demands that these children's stories continue to be told until we achieve our national commitment to a free *and* appropriate public education for all.

REFERENCES

Dewey, J. (1897). My pedagogic creed. *School Journal, 54,* 77–80. Retrieved from http://dewey.pragmatism.org/creed.htm

Education for All Handicapped Children Act of 1975, Pub. L. No. 94–142, 89 Stat. 773 (1975).

Eisner, E. W. (1988). The primacy of experience and the politics of method. *Educational Researcher, 17*(5), 15–20.

Fletcher, J. (2015). Overview and key findings. Retrieved from http://www.texasld-center.org/education-research-matters/item/november-2015

Friend, M. (2008). Co-teaching: A simple solution that isn't simple after all. *Journal of Curriculum and Instruction, 2*(2), 9–19.

Gewirtz, S. (2006). Towards a contextualized analysis of social justice in education. *Educational Philosophy and Theory, 38*(1), 69–81.

Harr-Robins, J., Song, M., Hurlburt, S., Pruce, C., Danielson, L., & Garet, M. (2013). *The inclusion of students with disabilities in school accountability systems: An update* (NCEE 2013-4017). Washington, DC: National Center for Education Evaluation and Regional Assistance, Institute of Education Sciences, U.S. Department of Education.

Imig, D. G., & Imig, S. R. (2006). The teacher effectiveness movement: How 80 years of essentialist control have shaped the teacher education profession. *Journal of Teacher Education, 57*(2), 167–180.

Individuals with Disabilities Education Improvement Act of 2004, 34 C.F.R. 300.1 *et seq.* (Electronic Code of Federal Regulations, 2017).

Klein, S. (2004). Reducing special education paperwork. *Principal, Sept./Oct.,* 58–60.

Leone, P., & Weinberg, L. (2012). Addressing the unmet educational needs of children and youth in the juvenile justice and child welfare systems. Center for Juvenile Justice Reform. Retrieved from https://cjjr.georgetown.edu/wp-content/uploads/2015/03/EducationalNeedsofChildrenandYouth_May2010.pdf

Morgan, P. L., Frisco, M., Farkas, G., & Hibel, J. (2010). A propensity score matching analysis of the effects of special education services. *Journal of Special Education, 43*(4), 236–254.

National Center for Learning Disabilities. (2014). *The state of learning disabilities* (3rd ed.). NY: Author.

No Child Left Behind Act of 2001, Pub. L. No. 107–110, 115 Stat. 1425 (2001).

Rosenthal, B. M. (2016). Denied: How Texas keeps tens of thousands of children out of special education. *Houston Chronicle*. Retrieved from http://www.houston-chronicle.com/denied/1/

Ryder, R. E. (2017, January 19). [Letter to Hon. Mike Morath]. U.S. Department of Education — Texas Listening Sessions documents. Retrieved from https://ed.gov/about/offices/list/osers/events/2016/texas-listening-sessions/files/letter-to-mike-morath--01-19-2017.pdf

Schwinn, P. (2016, November 2). [Letter to Assistant Secretary Swenson]. U.S. Department of Education – Texas Listening Sessions documents. Retrieved from https://www2.ed.gov/about/offices/list/osers/events/2016/texas-listening-sessions/files/tea-response-to-osersletter.pdf

Sullivan, A. L., & Proctor, S. (2016). The shield or the sword? Revising the debate on racial disproportionality in special education and implications for school psychologists. *School Psychology Forum: Research in Practice, 10*(3), 278-288.

Swenson, S. (2016, October 3). [Letter to Hon. Mike Morath]. U.S. Department of Education–Texas Listening Sessions documents. Retrieved from https://ed.gov/about/offices/list/osers/events/2016/texas-listening-sessions/files/letter-to-mike-morath-10-03-2016.pdf

Texas Education Agency. (2016). Texas Essential Knowledge and Skills for Kindergarten. Retrieved from http://tea.texas.gov/index2.aspx?id=6148

U.S. Department of Education. (2016). Teacher shortage areas nationwide listing 1990–1991 through 2016–2017. Retrieved from https://www2.ed.gov/about/offices/list/ope/pol/tsa.pdf

INDEX

A

Accommodations, 6, 43, 131, 133, 135, 136.

C

Cheramie's four questions approach, 26, 35, 39; application of, 30–32, 35–38.
Child Find mandate, 75.

D

Deficit view, 128, 160–161; of English language learners, 98, of students of color, 82.
Discrepancy model, 9, 21, 23, 25–26, 39.
Disproportionate representation, 74–76; causes of, 79–80, 82; and English language learners, 81, 93–95; and socioeconomic status, 76–77, 81; and students of color, 78–79, 81.

E

Education of All Handicapped Children Act, 5–6, 51–52, 60, 113, 178.
Education of the Handicapped Act, 4, 5–6, 22.
Elementary and Secondary Education Act, 4, 7, 8.
Emotional disturbance: definition of, 57–58.
English Language Learners, 93–94; assessment of, 95–96; effective programming for, 104–105, 106. *See also* Disproportionate representation
Evaluation for eligibility, 75, 85, 132; examples of, 30–38, 46–49, 65–67, 100–103; parents' role in, 9, 75, 113, 177; prob-

lems with, 40, 54, 76, 84. *See also* English language learners, assessment of
Every Student Succeeds Act, 9.

F

Free appropriate public education, 4, 5, 13, 52, 57, 113–114, 116, 130–131.

I

Individualized educational program, 5, 6, 112, 125, 13; compliance, 113–115; objectives in, 112–113, 115–117, 124.
Individuals with Disabilities Education Act, 7, 24, 52, 55, 87; and IEPs, 6, 113–115, 116–117, 122, 126.
Individuals with Disabilities Education Improvement Act, 8–9, 13, 24–25, 43, 57, 75, 78, 96, 112, 128, 155, 162, 177.
Least restrictive environment, 5, 10, 13, 178.
Luria method, 28.

M

Modifications: 43, 131, 133, 135, 136, 137.
Multi–Tiered Systems of Support, 167–168.

N

Narrative approach, 10–12.
No Child Left Behind Act, 7, 9, 94, 112, 116, 155, 180.

P

Parental rights and responsibilities, 5, 8, 9, 12,